CW00404681

SHEFFIELD/ROTHERHAM ATLAS

CONTENTS

©Geographia Ltd. Revised Edition 1987

ISBN 0 09 218060 4   EAL

The maps in this Atlas are based upon the Ordnance Survey Maps with the sanction of the Controller of H.M. Stationery Office, with additions obtained from Local Authorities. The Ordnance Survey is not responsible for the accuracy of the National Grid on this Production.

The representation on these maps of a Road, Track or Footpath is no evidence of the existence of a right of way.

The contents of this publication are believed correct at the time of printing. Nevertheless the Publishers can accept no responsibility for errors or omissions or for changes in the details given.

GEOGRAPHIA LTD. Duncan Street, Edinburgh EH9 1TA

KEY TO MAP PAGES

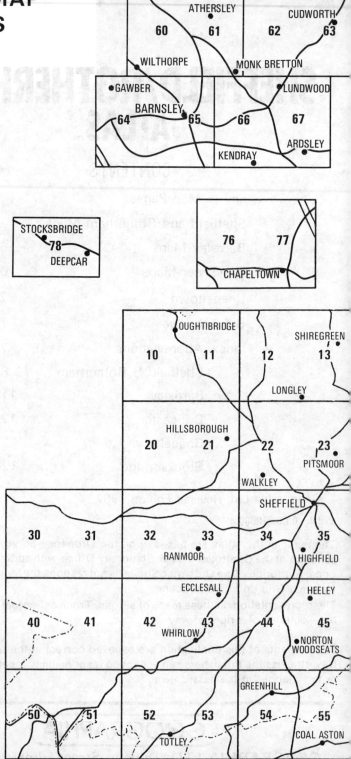

ATHERSLEY
CUDWORTH
60 61 62 63
WILTHORPE
MONK BRETTON
GAWBER LUNDWOOD
BARNSLEY
64 65 66 67
ARDSLEY
KENDRAY

STOCKSBRIDGE
78
DEEPCAR

76 77
CHAPELTOWN

OUGHTIBRIDGE
SHIREGREEN
10 11 12 13
LONGLEY
HILLSBOROUGH
20 21 22 23
PITSMOOR
WALKLEY
SHEFFIELD
30 31 32 33 34 35
RANMOOR
HIGHFIELD
ECCLESALL
HEELEY
40 41 42 43 44 45
WHIRLOW
NORTON
WOODSEATS
GREENHILL
50 51 52 53 54 55
COAL ASTON
TOTLEY

GEOGRAPHIA LTD. Duncan Street, Edinburgh EH9 1TA

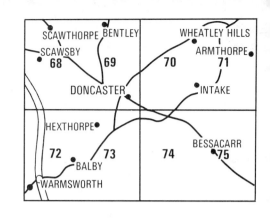

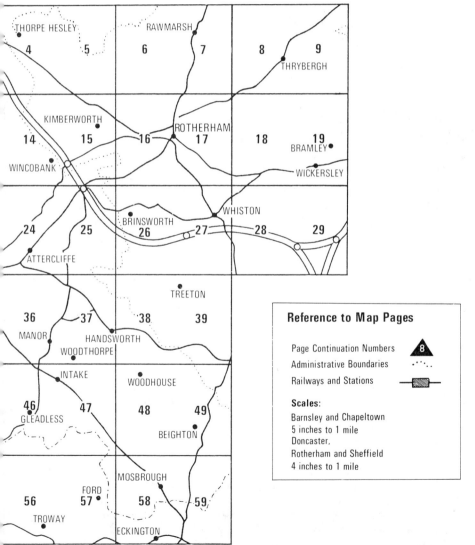

THORPE HESLEY

4 5 6 RAWMARSH 7 8 9 THRYBERGH

KIMBERWORTH

14 15 16 ROTHERHAM 17 18 19 BRAMLEY

WINCOBANK

24 25 BRINSWORTH 26 27 WHISTON 28 29

ATTERCLIFFE

TREETON

36 37 38 39

MANOR HANDSWORTH
WOODTHORPE

INTAKE WOODHOUSE

46 47 48 49

GLEADLESS BEIGHTON

MOSBROUGH

FORD
56 57 58 59

TROWAY

ECKINGTON

Reference to Map Pages

Page Continuation Numbers   **8**

Administrative Boundaries   ·.··..

Railways and Stations   ▨

Scales:

Barnsley and Chapeltown
5 inches to 1 mile
Doncaster,
Rotherham and Sheffield
4 inches to 1 mile

SCAWTHORPE BENTLEY WHEATLEY HILLS ARMTHORPE

SCAWSBY
68 69 70 71

DONCASTER INTAKE

HEXTHORPE

72 73 74 BESSACARR 75

BALBY

WARMSWORTH

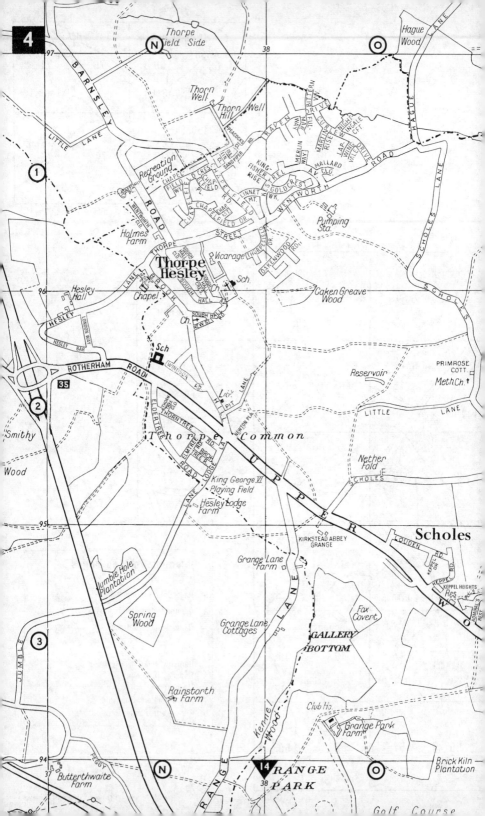

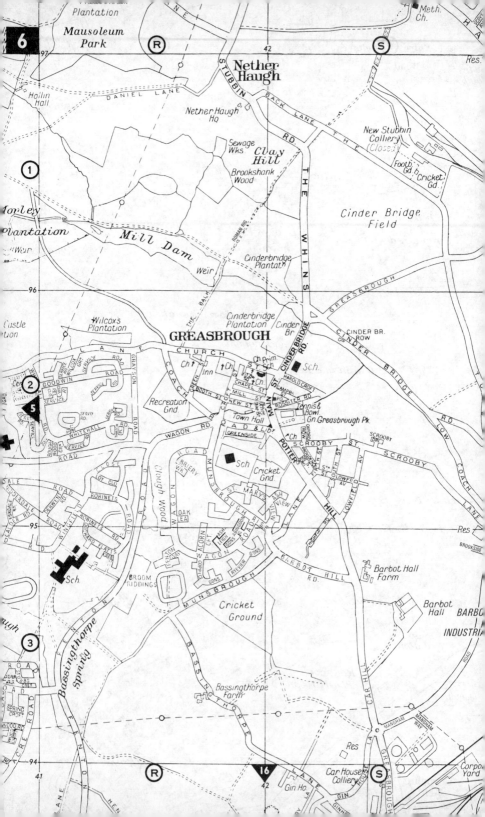

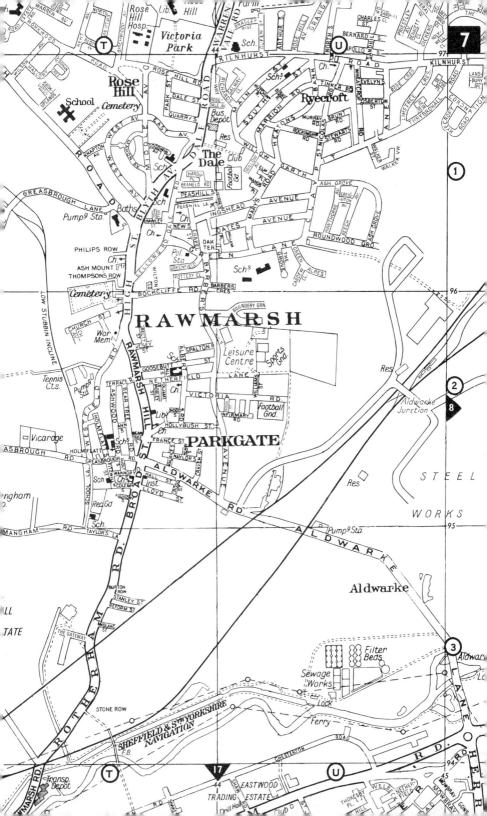

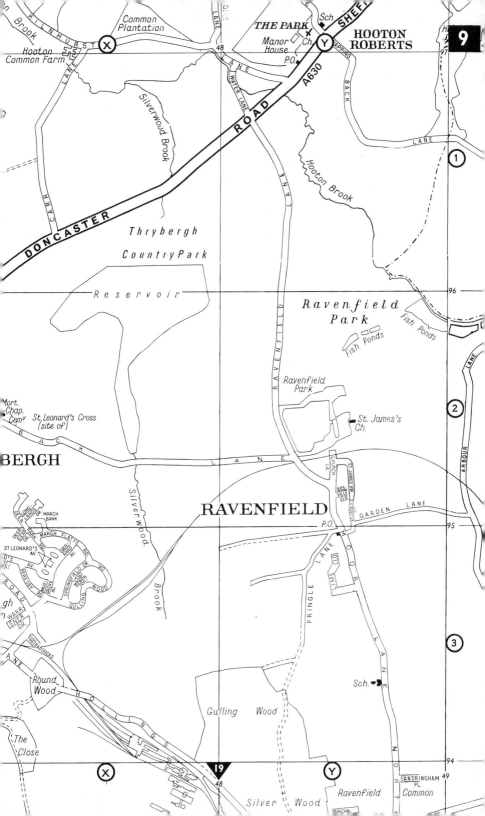

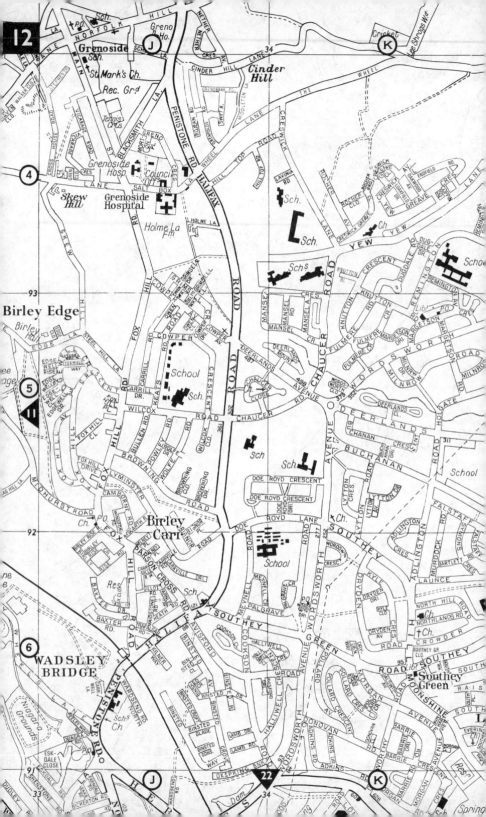

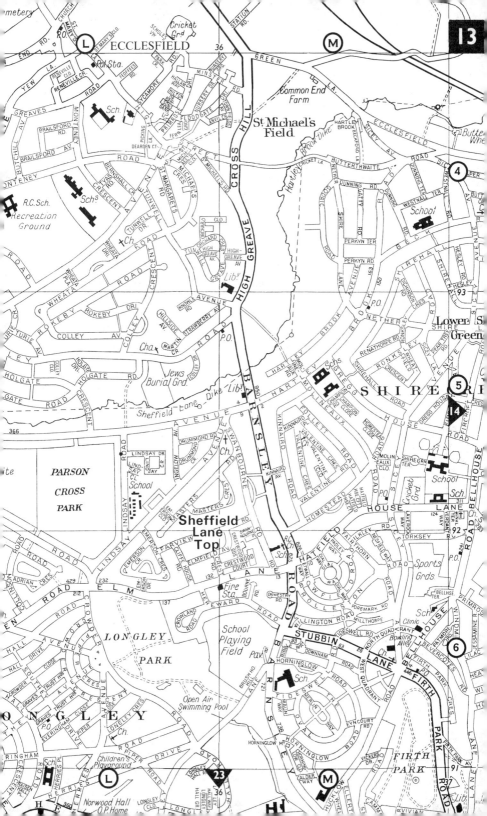

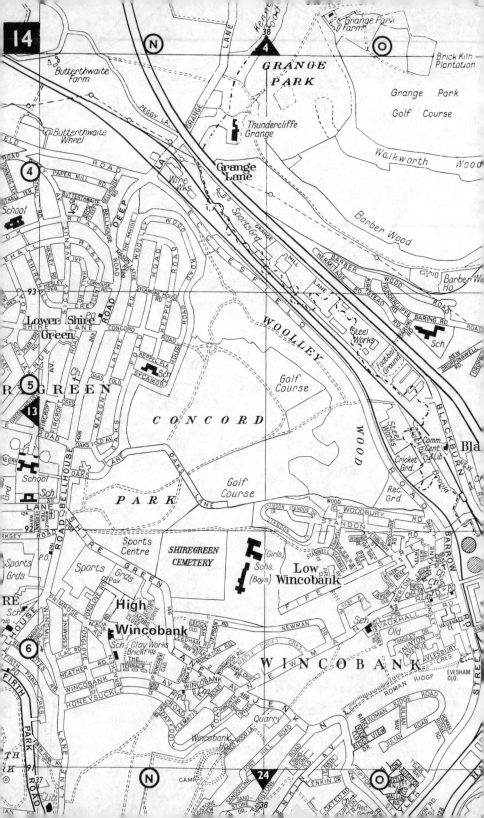

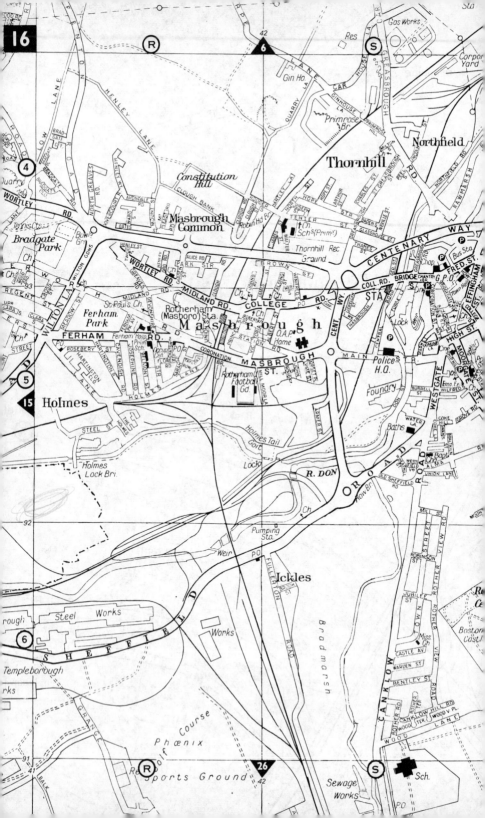

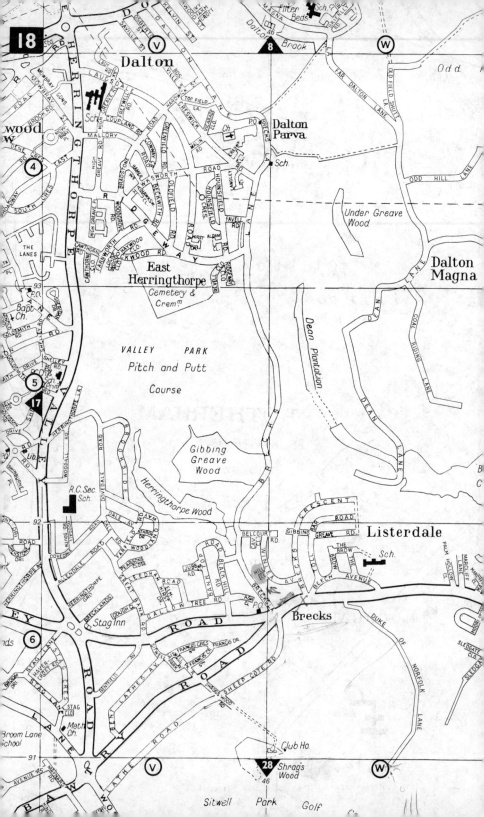

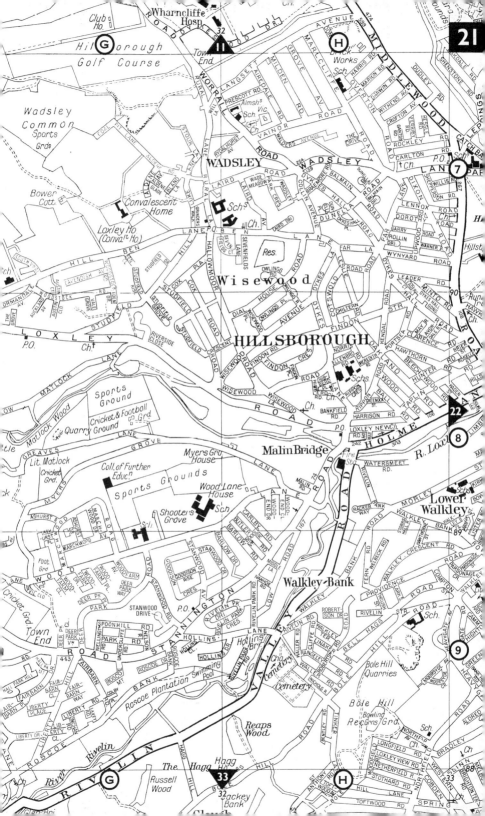

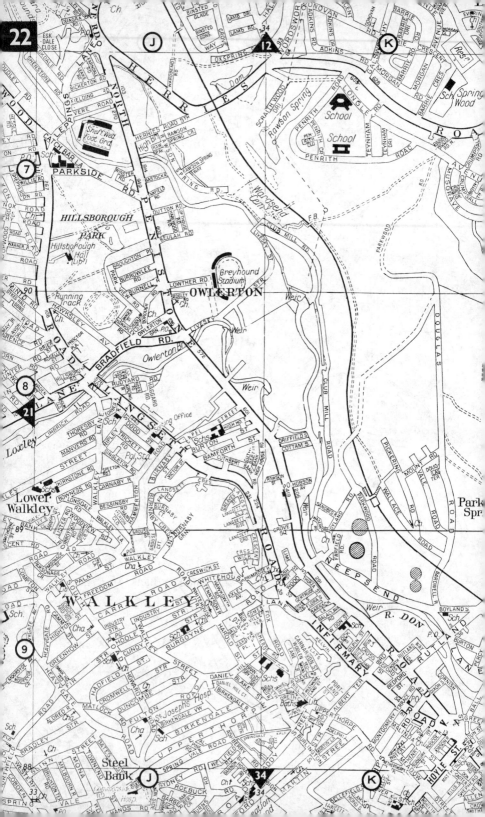

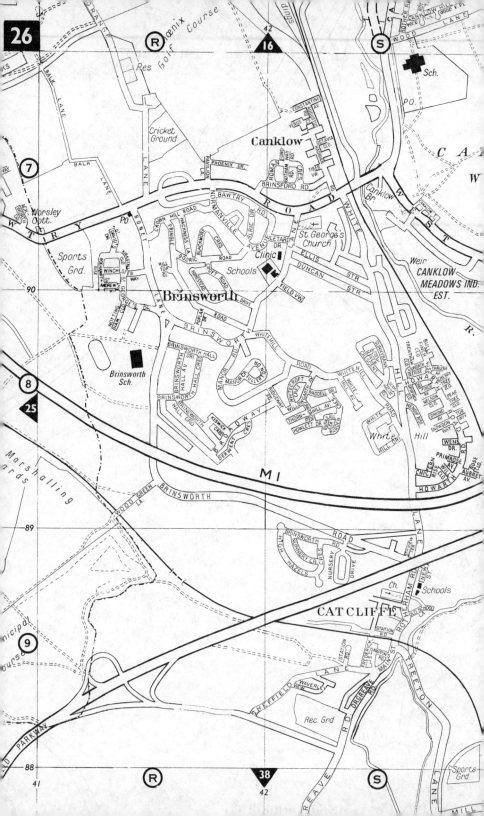

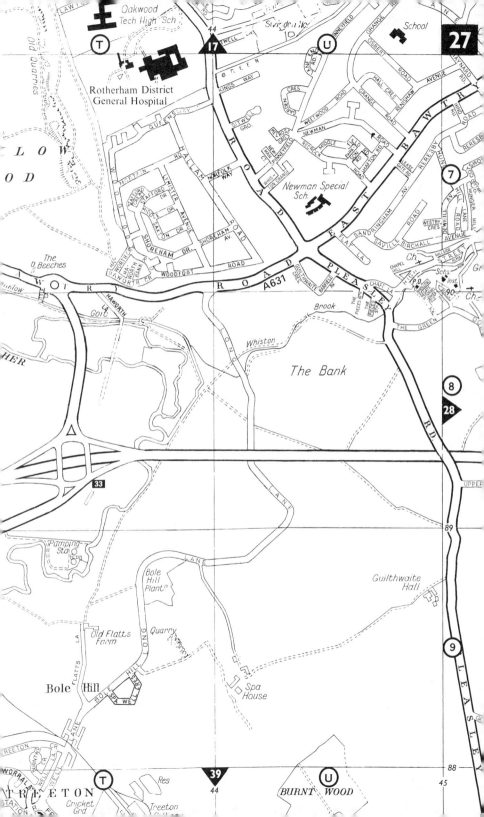

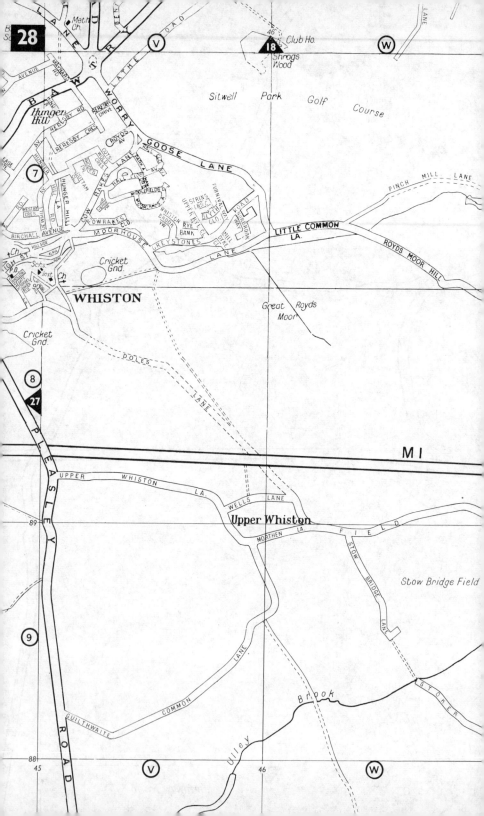

29

X

Y

GILLOTT LA.

HOLLOW IN LANE

FIRST LANE

QUARRY FIELD LANE

48

19

R.M.INJ. GRADE

ROAD

SPRINGVALE CL.

NEWHALL AV.

NETHERMOOR DR.

SECOND LANE

MORTHEN

Kings Pond Plant.

FLAT LANE

SANDY

7

Pinch Mill Brook

Liner Wood

MOAT LANE

GREEN LANE

KINGSFORTH LA.

ROAD

90

KINGSFORTH LA.

YORK LANE

8

Morthen

WOOD-HOUSE GRN.

ROWENA DRIVE

KATHERINE AV.

BRAMPTON DR.

CROSS

LETHAL S.

89

Morthen Brook

LANE

THURCROFT

LOCKSLEY

WITHOLD

MORTHEN CL.

ULRICA DR.

ROWENA

IVANHOE RD.

ATHELSTANE CRES.

ZAMOR

9

Grange Fm.

BRAMPTON CL. CO.

MEL-ROSE CL.

BRAMPTON

Brampton en le Morthen

ROAD

WOOD LA.

LANE

COMMON LANE

88

X

Y

BRAMPTON

48

49

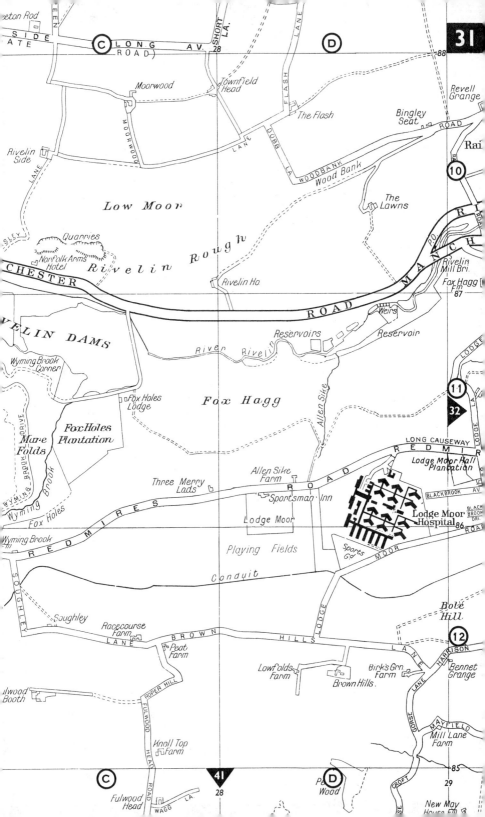

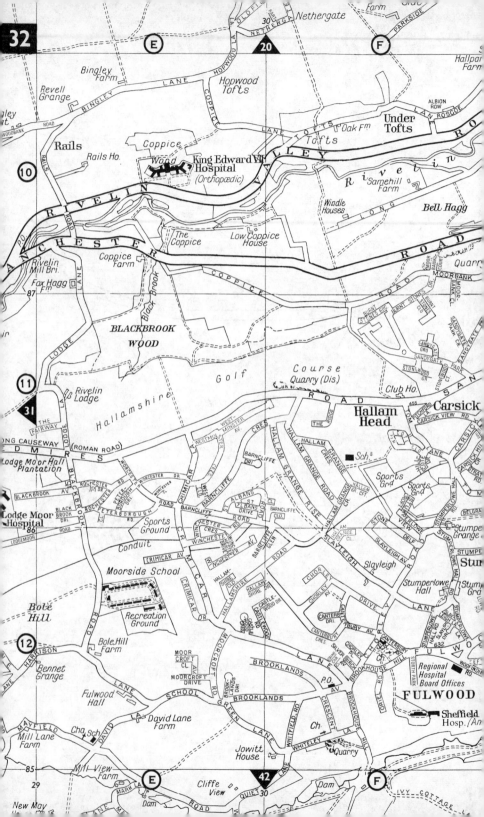

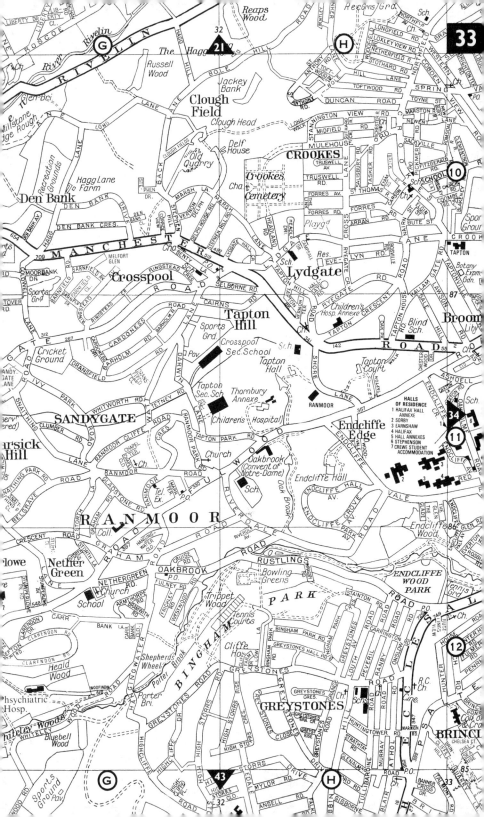

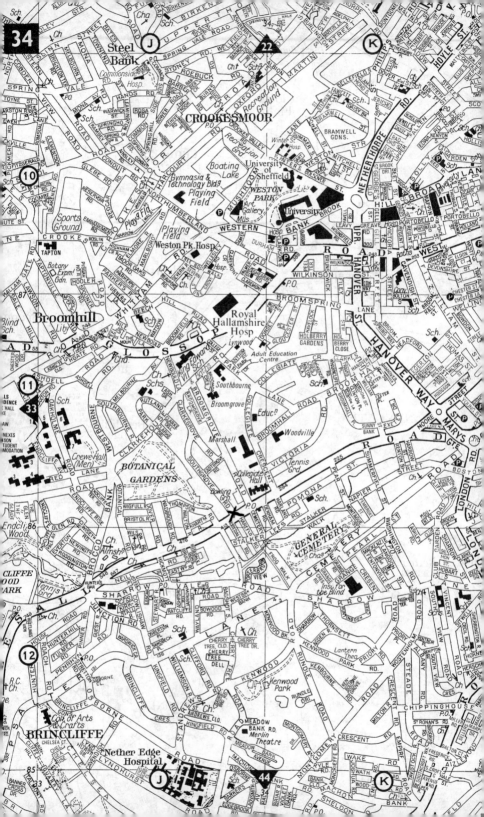

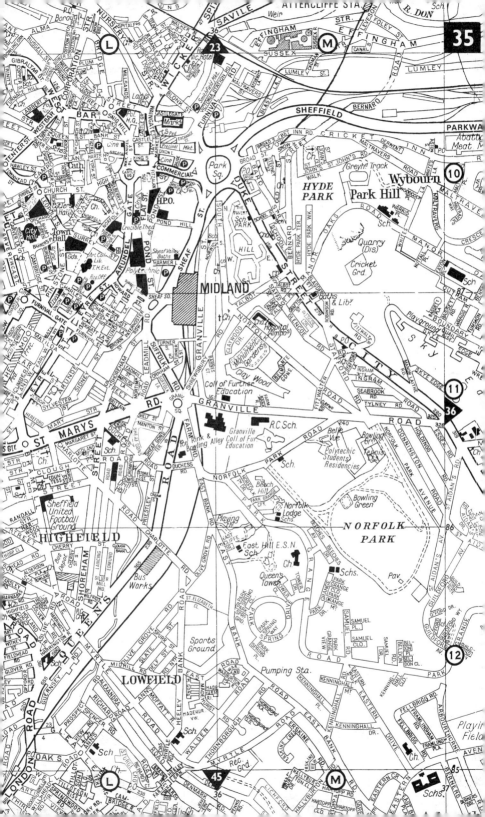

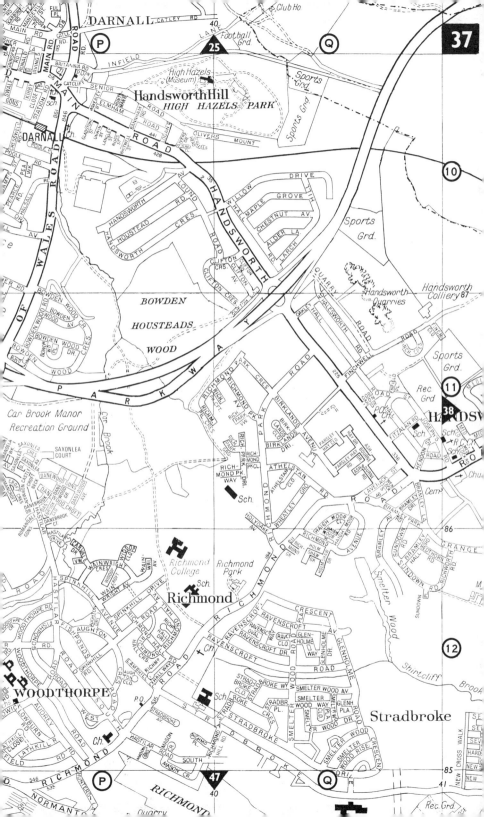

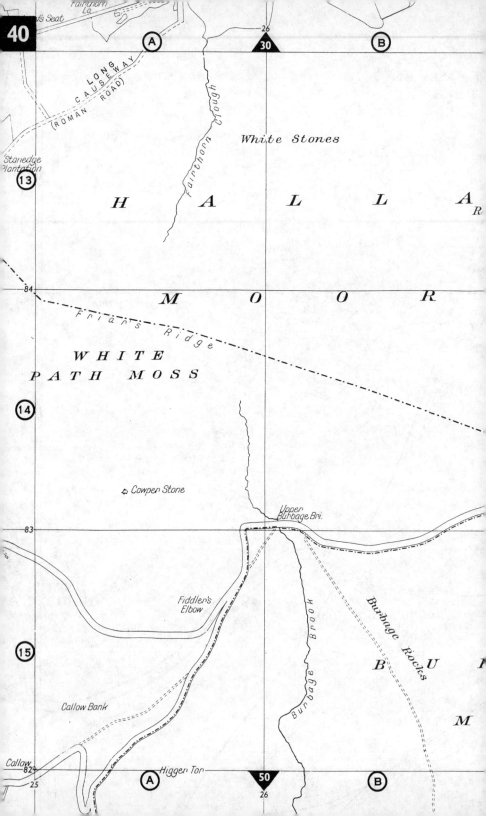

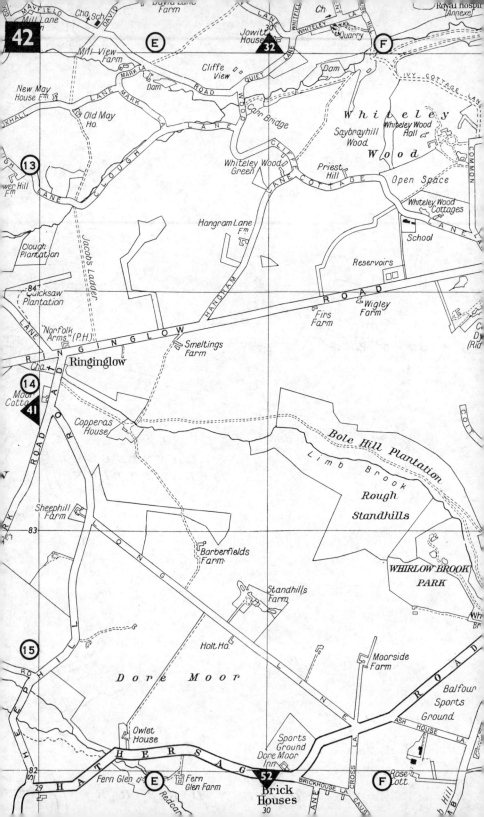

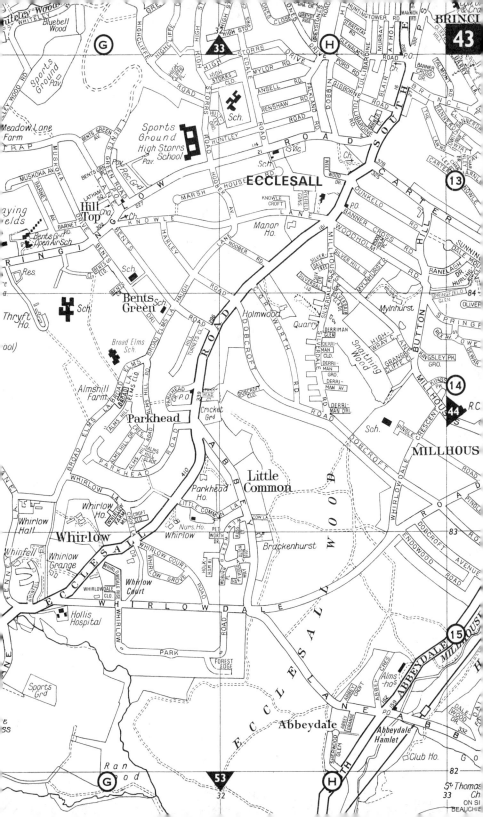

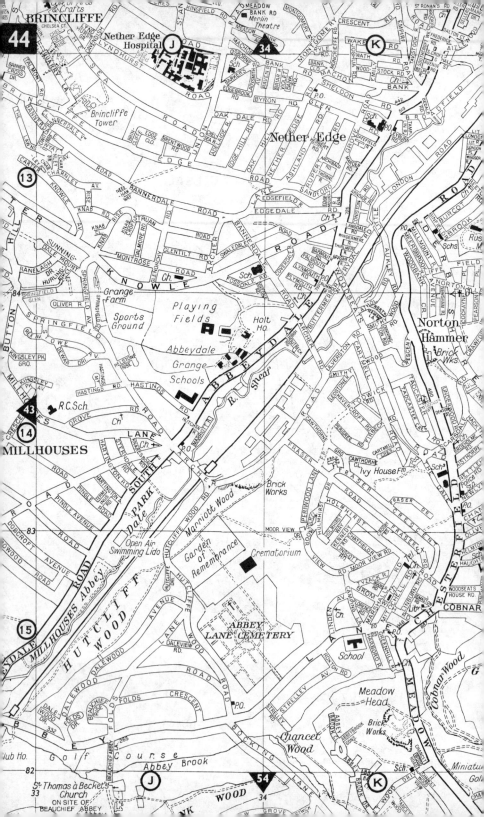

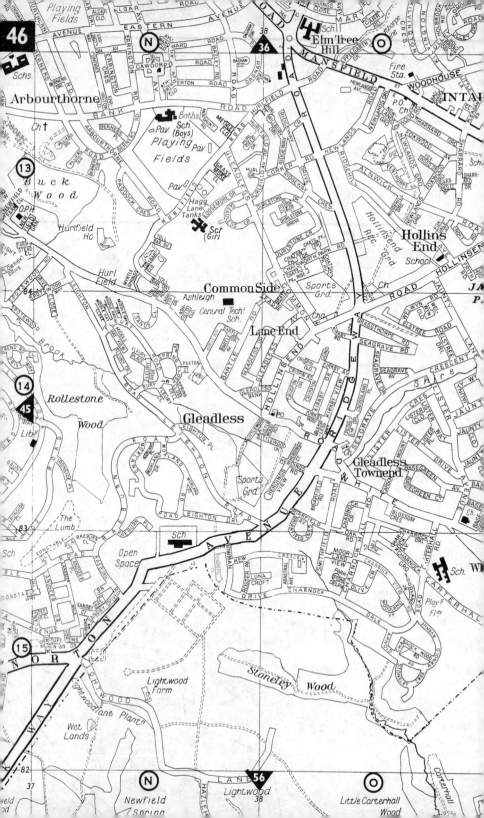

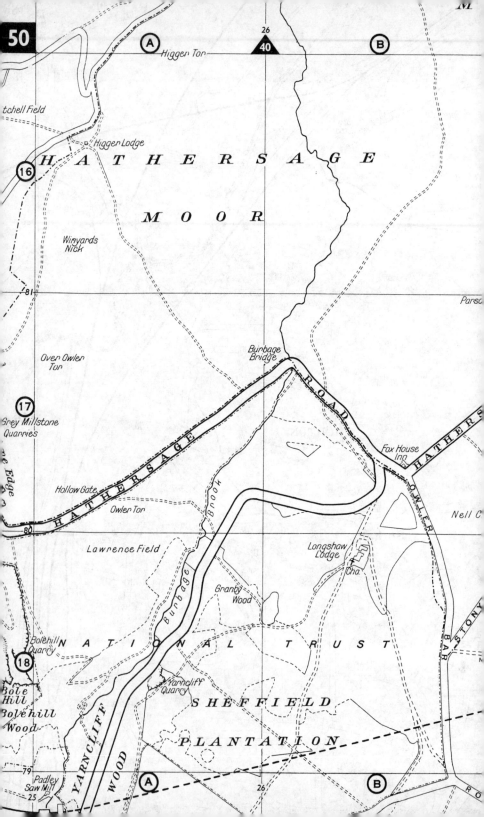

M

Higgen Tor

tchell Field

Higgen Lodge

16

H A T H E R S A G E

M O O R

Winyards Nick

81

Over Owler Tor

Burbage Bridge

17

Grey Millstone Quarries

ROAD

HATHERS

Fox House Inn

e Edge

HATHERSAGE

Hollow Gate

Owler Tor

Brook

80

Parso

Nell C

OWLER

Lawrence Field

Burbage

Longshaw Lodge

Cha.

Granby Wood

N A T I O N A L   T R U S T

Bolehill Quarry

18

S T O N Y

B A R

Bole Hill

Yarncliff Quarry

Bolehill Wood

S H E F F I E L D

YARNCLIFF   WOOD

P L A N T A T I O N

79

Ⓐ

26

Ⓑ

R

Padley Saw Mill

25

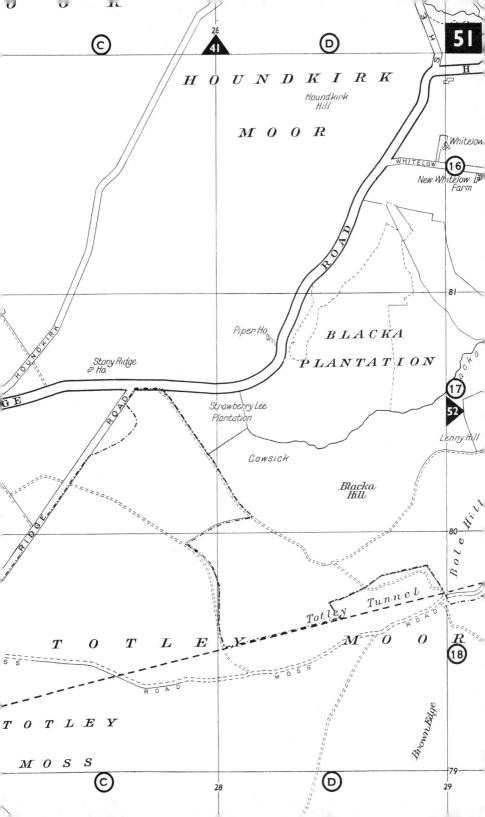

HOUNDKIRK

Houndkirk
Hill

MOOR

Whitelow

WHITELOW 16

New Whitelow
Farm

81

ROAD

Piper Ho.

BLACKA

Stony Ridge
& Ho.

PLANTATION

Blacka

17

RIDGE

ROAD

Strawberry Lee
Plantation

52

Lenny Hill

HOUNDKIRK

Cowsick

Blacka
Hill

80

Bole Hill

Totley Tunnel

ROAD

TOTLEY

MOOR

R

18

SS

MOSS

ROAD

Brown Edge

TOTLEY

MOSS

79

28

29

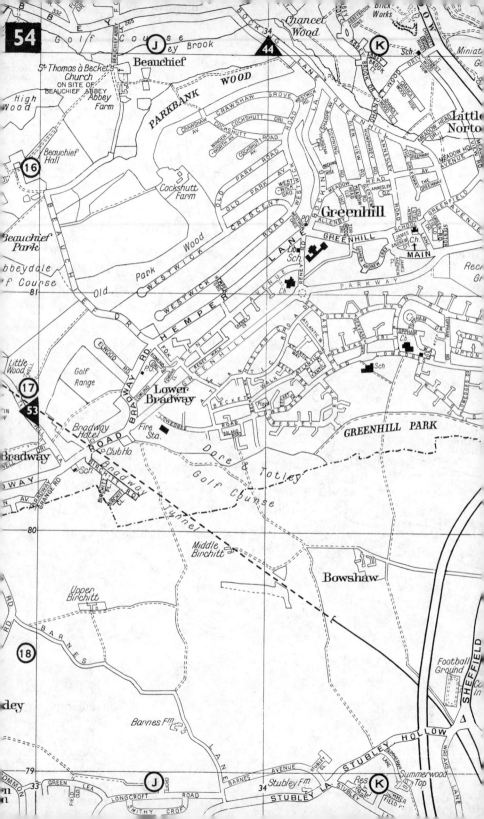

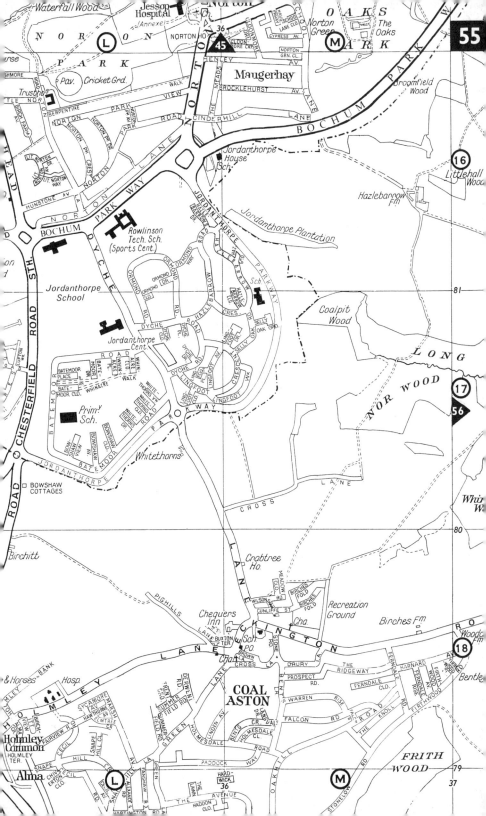

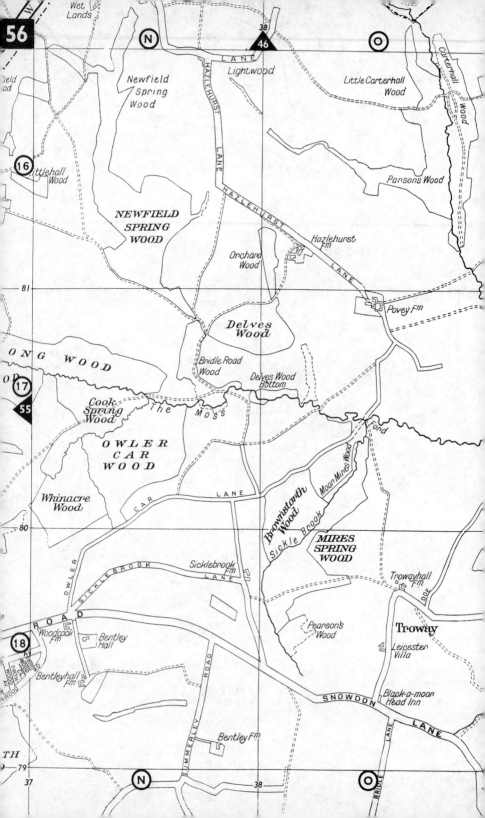

W

Wet Lands

16

Newfield Spring Wood

ttlehall Wood

Hazlehurst Lane

N

Lightwood

38
46

Little Carterhall Wood

Carterhall Wood

⊙

Pansons Wood

NEWFIELD SPRING WOOD

HAZLEHURST LANE

Hazlehurst Fm

Orchard Wood

81

Delves Wood

Povey Fm

ONG WOOD

OP

17

55

Cook Spring Wood

Bridle Road Wood

The Moss

Delves Wood Bottom

Pond

OWLER CAR WOOD

Whinacre Wood

CAR LANE

Brownstorth Wood

Moon Mires Wood

Sickle Brook

MIRES SPRING WOOD

80

OWLER

SICKLEBROOK

Sicklebrook Fm

LANE

Trowayhall Fm

DOE

Troway

18

Woodcock Fm

Bentley Hall

Pearson's Wood

Leicester Villa

ROAD

Bentleyhall Fm

SUMMERLEY ROAD

Bentley Fm

SNOWDON LANE

Black-a-moon Head Inn

LANE

BRIDLE

TH

79

37

N

38

⊙

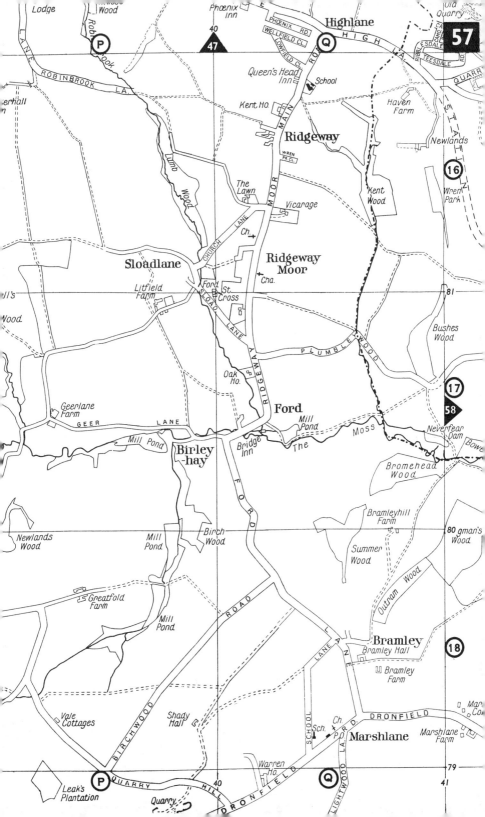

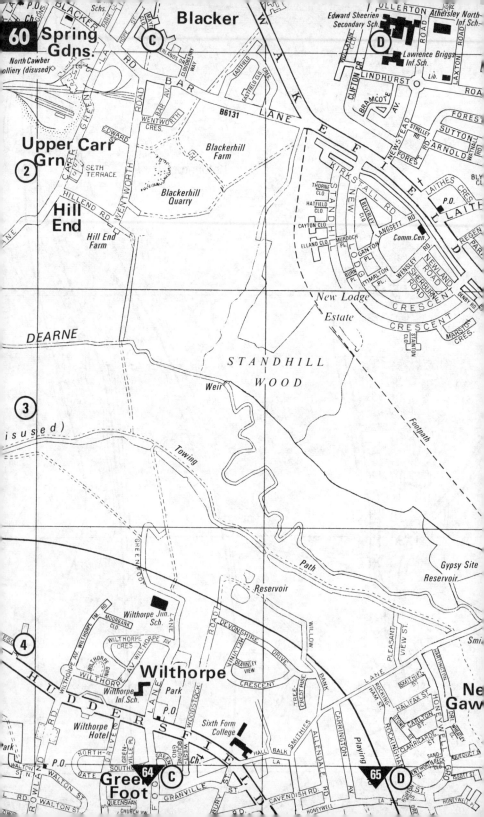

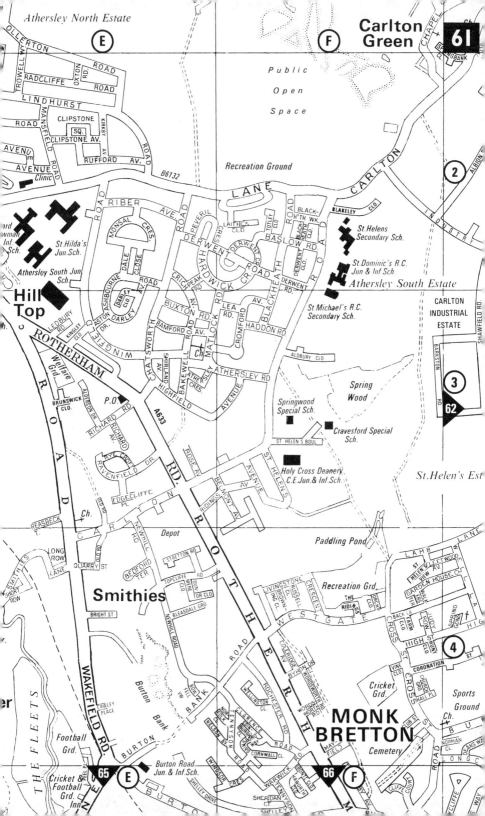

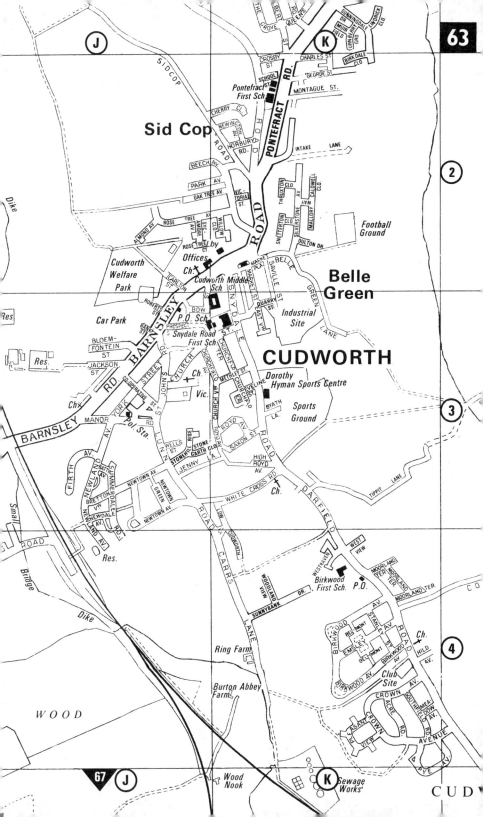

BARNSLEY

65

Old Mill

Harborough Hill

Queen's Recreation Ground

Sports Grd.

Oakwell Grd. (Barnsley F.C.)

Beevor Court

Barnsley Cemetery

Pindar Oaks (Day Hosp.)

Bus Depot

Worsbrough Common

Mount Vernon Special Sch.

Worsbrough Common

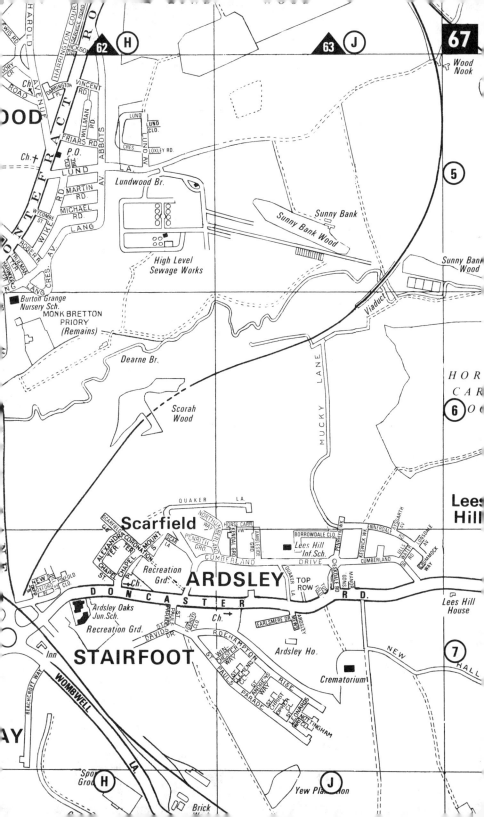

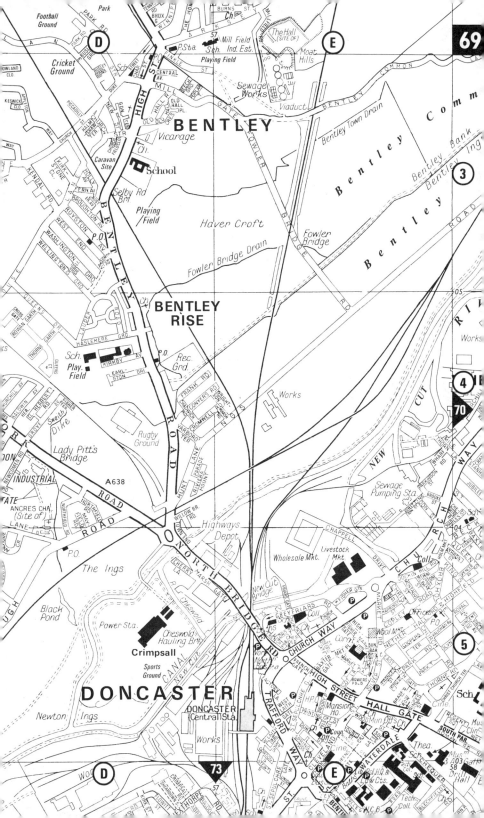

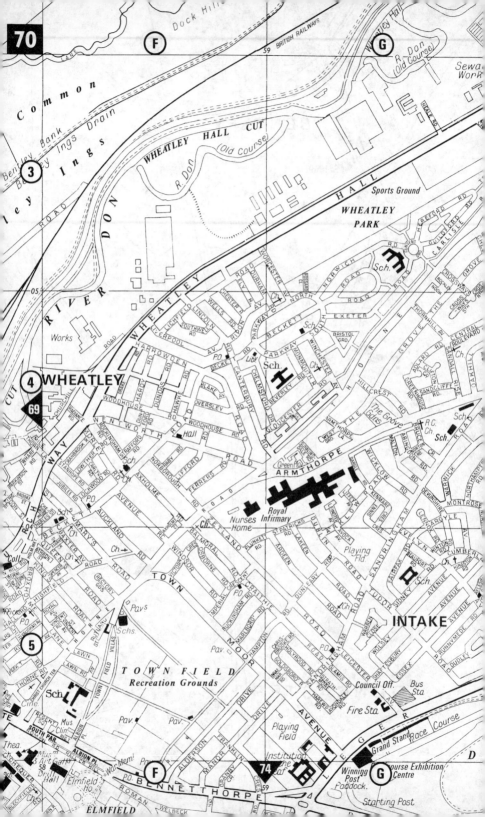

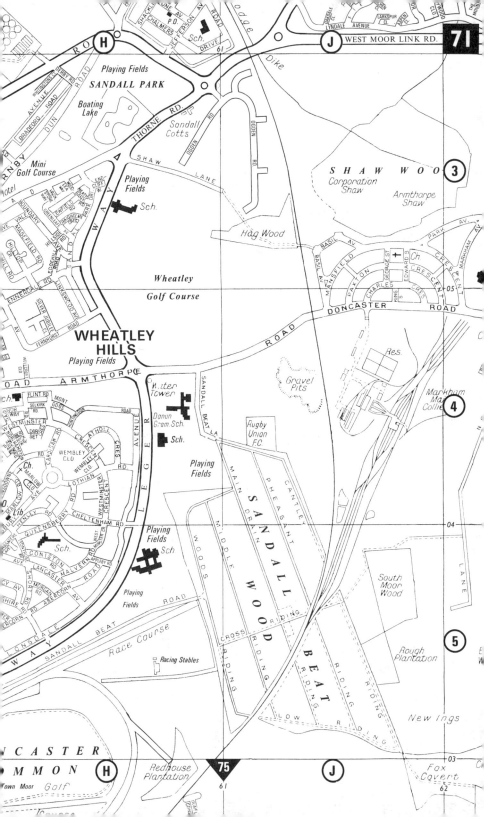

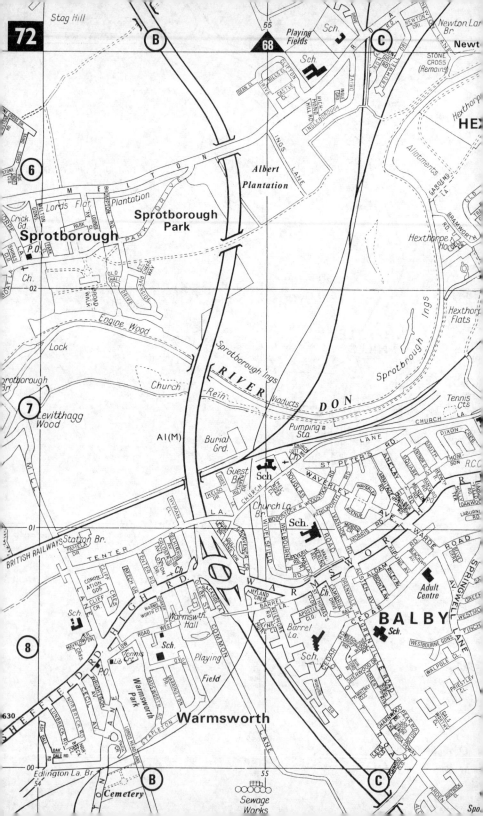

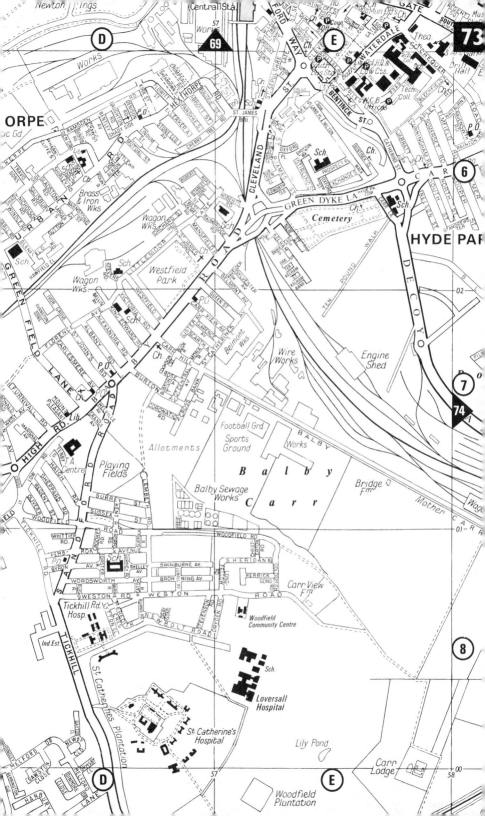

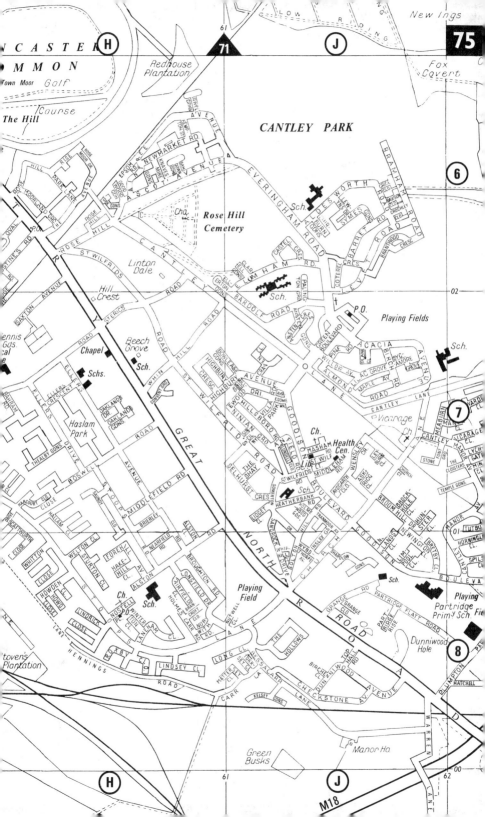

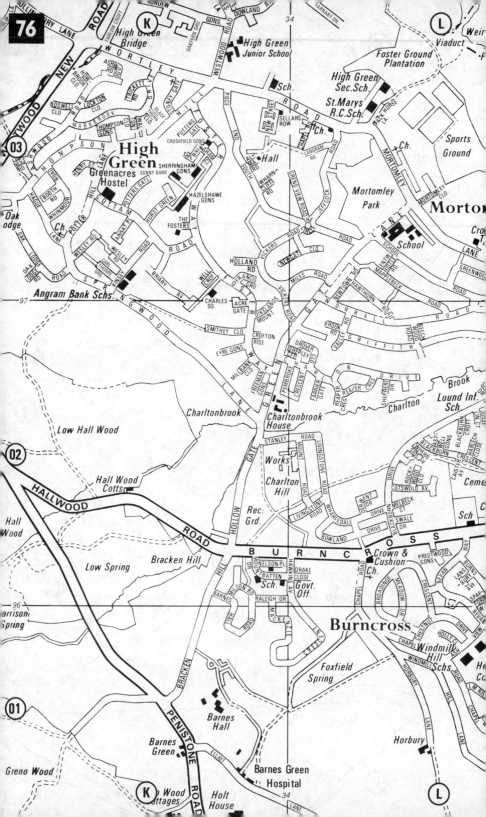

INDEX TO STREETS

District Abbreviations

Aug.	Aughton	Greas.	Greasbrough	Ridg.	Ridgeway
Btn.	Beighton	Gren.	Grenoside	Ring.	Ringinglow
Black.	Blackburn	Hack.	Hackenthorpe	Roth.	Rotherham
Brad.	Bradfield	Hol.	Holbrook	Sch.	Scholes
Bradw.	Bradway	Hoot.R.	Hooton Roberts	Shef.	Sheffield
Bram.	Bramley	Killa.	Killamarsh	Stan.	Stannington
Bram.M.	Brampton en le Morthen	Kiln.	Kilnhurst	Swall.	Swallownest
Brin.	Brinsworth	Kimb.	Kimberworth	Th.Hes.	Thorpe Hesley
Cank.	Canklow	Lox.	Loxley	Thry.	Thrybergh
Cat.	Catcliffe	Marsh.	Marshlane	Thur.	Thurcroft
C.A.	Coal Aston	May.	Mayfield	Tot.	Totley Rise
Dal.M.	Dalton Magna	Mor.	Morthen	Tree.	Treeton
Dron.	Dronfield	Mosb.	Mosbrough	Wd.M.	Woodhouse Mill
D.Wd.	Dronfield Woodhouse	Ought.	Oughtibridge	Whis.	Whiston
Dun.	Dungworth	Park.	Parkgate	Wick.	Wickersley
Eccl.	Ecclesall	Rav.	Ravenfield	Wood.	Woodhouse
Eck.	Eckington	Raw.	Rawmarsh	Wor.	Worrall

General Abbreviations

All.	Alley	Ct.	Court	Mans.	Mansions	S.	South
App.	Approach	Dr.	Drive	Mkt.	Market	Sq.	Square
Arc.	Arcade	E.	East	Ms.	Mews	Sta.	Station
Av.	Avenue	Est.	Estate	Mt.	Mount	St.	Street
Bldgs.	Buildings	Esp.	Esplanade	N.	North	Ter.	Terrace
Boul.	Boulevard	Gdns.	Gardens	Par.	Parade	Vills.	Villas
Bri.	Bridge	Gra.	Grange	Pass.	Passage	Vw.	View
Circ.	Circus	Grn.	Green	Pk.	Park	W.	West
Cft.	Croft	Gro.	Grove	Pl.	Place	Wf.	Wharf
Clo.	Close	Ho.	House	Prom.	Promenade	Wk.	Walk
Cor.St	Corner	Ind.	Industrial	Quad.	Quadrant	Yd.	Yard
Cotts.	Cottages	La.	Lane	Ri.	Rise		
Cres.	Crescent	Lo.	Lodge	Rd.	Road		

NOTES

The figures and letters following a street name indicate the postal district, map square and page where the name can be found. Thus Abbey Brook Clo. is in Sheffield postal district 8, in map square K15 on page 44.
A street name followed by the name of another street in italics does not appear on the map, but will be found adjoining or near the latter.

Name	Grid	Page
Abbey Brook Clo. 8	K15	44
Abbey Brook Ct. 8	K15	44
Abbey Brook Dr. 8	K15	44
Abbey Brook Gdns. 8	K15	44
Abbey Cres. 7	H15	43
Abbey Croft 7	H15	43
Abbey Grange 7	H15	43
Abbey La. 7, 8 & 11	G14	43
Abbey View Dr. 8	L14	45
Abbey View Rd. 8	L14	45
Abbeydale Park Cres. 17	G17	53
Abbeydale Park Ri. 17	G16	53
Abbeydale Rd. 7	J14	44
Abbeydale Rd. S. 7 & 17	G17	53
Abbeyfield Rd. 4	L8	23
Abell St., Thry. 65	W3	8
Abingdon Gdns., Roth. 61	R2	6
Abney Clo. 14	M13	45
Abney Dr. 14	M13	45
Abney Rd. 14	M13	45
Acacia Av., Bram. 66	Y5	19
Acacia Rd. 5	N6	14
Ackworth Dr. 9	Q7	25
Acorn Croft, Roth. 61	R3	6
Acorn Dr., Stan. 6	E8	20
Acorn Hill, Stan. 6	F8	20
Acorn St. 3	L9	23
Acorn Way, Stan. 6	E9	20
Acre La., Ought. 30	E4	10
Acres Hill La. 9	O10	36
Acres Hill Rd. 9	P10	37
Adastral Av. 12	O15	46
Adby Rd., Roth. 61	P3	5
Addison Rd. 5	M7	23
Addy Clo. 6	K9	22
Addy Dr. 6	J9	22
Addy St. 6	K9	22
Adelaide Rd. 7	J13	44
Adelphi St. 6	K9	22
Adkins Dr. 5	K6	12
Adkins Rd. 5	K6	12
Adlington Cres. 5	K6	12
Adlington Rd. 5	K6	12
Admirals Crest, Sch. 61	O3	4
Adrian Cres. 5	L6	13
Agden Rd. 7	K12	34
Ainsley Rd. 10	J10	34
Ainsty Rd. 7	K12	34
South View Cres.		
Air Mount Clo., Wick. 66	X6	19
Airedale Rd. 6	H7	21
Aireton Clo., Wick. 66	X5	19
Aisthorpe Rd. 8	K14	44
Aizlewood Rd. 8	K12	34
Akley Bank Clo. 17	G17	53
Albanus Cft., Stan. 6	F8	20
Acorn Dr.		
Albanus Ridge, Stan. 6	F9	20
Albany Rd. 7	K12	34
Albany St., Roth. 65	T5	17
Albert Rd. 12	S14	48
Albert Rd. 8	L13	45
Albert Rd., Raw. 62	T2	7
Albert St., Roth. 60	S5	16
Albert Terrace Rd. 6	K9	22
Albion Rd., Roth. 60	T5	17
Albion Row 6	F10	32
Albion St. 6	K10	34
Albion Yd. 2	K11	34
London Rd.		
Alcester Rd. 7	K12	34
Tavistock Rd.		
Aldam Clo. 17	G18	53
Aldam Clo., Roth. 65	V4	18
Aldam Croft 17	G18	53
Aldam Rd. 17	G18	53
Aldam Way 17	G18	53
Aldene Av. 6	G7	21
Aldene Glade 6	G7	21
Aldene Rd. 6	G7	21
Alder La. 9	Q10	37
Alderney Rd. 2	L12	35
Queens Rd.		
Alders Grn., Lox. 6	F7	20
Alderson Pl. 2	L12	35
Alderson Rd. 2	L12	35
Alderson Rd. N. 2	L12	35
Alderson Rd.		
Aldfield Way 5	L7	23
Aldine Ct. 1	L10	35
High St.		
Aldred Clo., Wick. 66	X5	19
Aldred Rd. 10	J9	22
Aldred St., Roth. 65	T5	17
Aldwarke La., Aldwarke 65	U3	7
Aldwarke Rd., Raw. 62	T2	7
Alexandra Clo., Roth. 61	Q4	15
Alexandra Rd. 2	L12	35
Alexandra Rd., Swall. 31	V12	39
Alexandra Rd., Dron. 18	L18	55
Alford Av. 30	F4	10
Alfred Rd. 9	N8	24
Algar Clo. 2	N12	36
Algar Cres. 2	N12	36
Algar Dr. 2	N12	36
Algar Pl. 2	N12	36
Algar Rd. 2	N12	36
Alice Rd., Roth. 61	R4	16
Alison Cres. 2	O11	36
All Saints Sq., Roth. 60	S5	16
Allan St., Roth. 65	T5	17
Allen Rd. 19	T15	49
Allen St. 3	K10	34
Allenby Dr. 8	K16	54
Allendale Rd., Roth. 65	V6	18
Allende Way 9	O9	24
Alliance St. 4	M8	23
Allt St. 62	T2	7
Alma Cres., Dron. 18	L18	55
Alma Rd., Roth. 60	S5	16
Alma Row, Whis. 60	V7	28
Alma St. 3	L9	23
Almond Glade, Wick. 66	Y6	19
Alms Hill Cres. 11	G14	43
Alms Hill Dr. 11	G14	43
Alms Hill Glade 11	G14	43
Alms Hill Rd. 11	G14	43
Alney Pl. 6	J6	12
Alnwick Dr. 12	O13	46
Alnwick Rd. 12	O13	46
Alpha Rd., Roth. 65	U4	17
Alpine Rd. 6	J9	22
Alport Av. 14	Q13	47
Alport Dr. 14	Q13	47
Alport Gro. 14	Q13	47
Alport Pl. 14	Q13	47
Alport Rd. 12	Q13	47
Alric Dr., Brin. 60	R7	26
Alsing Rd. 9	P6	15
Alton Clo. 11	H15	43
Amberley St. 2	O8	24
Ambleside Clo. 19	T17	59
Amos Rd. 9	O7	24
Andover Dr. 3	L9	23
Andover St. 3	L9	23
Andrew La. 3	L9	23
Wicker La.		
Andrew St. 3	L9	23
Andwell La. 10	D13	41
Angel St. 3	L10	35
Angerford Av. 8	L14	45
Ann St. 62	T2	7
Annesley Clo. 8	K16	54
Annesley Rd. 8	K16	54
Anns Rd. 2	L12	35
Anns Rd. N. 2	L12	35
Ansell Rd. 11	H13	43
Antrim Av. 10	J11	34
Anvil Clo. 6	G9	21
Anvil Cres., Eccl. 30	L4	13
Apollo St., Raw. 62	U1	7
Applegarth Clo. 12	O12	36
Applegarth Dr. 12	O13	36
Arbour La., Rav. 65	Y2	9
Arbourthorne Rd. 2	N13	46
Archdale Clo. 2	O12	36
Archdale Pl. 2	O12	36
Archdale Rd. 2	O11	36
Archer Gate, Lox. 6	F7	20
Archer La. 7	J13	44
Archer Rd. 8	K14	44
Archery Clo., Wick. 66	X6	19
Sorby Way		
Archibald Rd. 7	K13	44
Ardmore St. 9	O9	24
Ardsley Clo. 19	Q15	47
Ardsley Dr. 19	Q15	47
Ardsley Gro. 19	Q15	47
Ardsley Clo.		
Argyle Clo. 8	L13	45
Argyle Rd. 8	L13	45
Arley St. 2	L11	35
Armer St., Roth. 10	S5	16
Armley Rd. 9	O8	24
Arms Park Dr. 19	T17	59
Armstead Rd., Btn. 19	U14	49
Armthorpe Rd. 11	G12	33
Arnold Av. 12	O15	46
Arnold Rd., Roth. 65	U5	17
Arnold St. 6	J8	22
Arnside Rd. 8	K13	44
Arnside Ter. 8	K13	44
Arnside Rd.		
Arran Hill, Thry. 65	W2	8
Arran Rd. 10	H10	33
Arras St. 9	N9	24
Arthington St. 8	L13	45
Arthur St., Raw. 62	U1	7
Arthur St., Roth. 60	S4	16
Artisan Vw. 8	L13	45
Arundel Av., Dal.M. 65	V3	8
Arundel Av., Tree. 60	T10	39
Arundel Cotts., Tree. 60	T10	39
Arundel Cres., Tree. 60	T10	39
Arundel Gate 1	L10	35
Arundel La. 1	L11	35
Arundel Rd., Tree. 60	T10	39
Arundel St. 1	L11	35
Arundel St., Tree. 60	T10	39
Ascot St. 2	L11	35
Bramall La.		
Ash Clo., Roth. 65	V6	18
Ash Gro. 10	J11	34
Ash Gro., Raw. 62	U1	7
Ash Gro., Wick. 66	Y5	19
Ash House La. 17	F15	42
Ash Mt., Raw. 62	T1	7
Ash St. 6	K9	22
Ash St., Mosb. 19	S16	58
Ash View, Roth. 61	S2	6
Ashberry Rd. 6	J9	22
Ashbourne Gro. 13	Q11	37
Ashbourne Gro., Ought. 30	G5	11
Ashbourne Rd. 13	Q11	37
Ashbury Dr. 8	M15	45
Ashbury La. 8	M15	45
Ashdell 10	J11	34
Ashdell La. 10	J11	34
Ashdell Rd.		
Ashdell Rd. 10	J11	34
Ashdown Gdns. 19	U14	49
Asher Rd. 7	K12	34
South View Rd.		
Ashfield Clo. 12	N14	46
Ashfield Dr. 12	N14	46
Ashfield Dr. 14	N14	46
Ashford Rd. 11	J12	34
Ashfurlong Clo. 17	G16	53
Ashfurlong Dr. 17	G16	53

Ashfurlong Rd. 17	G16	53
Ashgate Clo. 10	J11	34
Ashgate La. 10	J11	34
Ashgate Rd.		
Ashgate Rd. 10	J11	34
Ashland Rd. 7	K13	44
Ashleigh Gdns., Roth. 61	R3	6
Ashley Rd. 11	K12	34
Ashmore Av., Eck. 31	R18	58
Ashpool Clo. 13	R13	48
Ashpool Clo., Wood. 13	R13	48
Ashurst Clo. 6	G8	21
Ashurst Dr. 6	G8	21
Ashurst Pl. 6	G9	21
Ashurst Rd. 6	G8	21
Ashwell Rd. 13	R13	48
Ashwood Rd. 62	T2	7
Ashworth Dr., Roth. 61	P3	5
Asline Rd. 2	L12	35
Asquith Rd. 9	O6	14
Barrow Rd.		
Aster Clo. 19	T14	49
Aston St. 2	M10	35
Athelstan Clo. 13	Q11	37
Athelstan Rd. 13	Q11	37
Athelstane Cres., Thur. 66	Y9	29
Athersley Gdns. 19	R15	48
Atherton Clo. 2	N13	46
Atherton Rd. 2	N13	46
Athol Rd. 8	K14	44
Athron Dr., Roth. 65	V6	18
Atkin Pl. 2	L12	35
St. Barnabas Rd.		
Atlantic Cres. 8	K17	54
Atlantic Dr. 8	K17	54
Atlantic Rd. 8	J17	54
Atlantic Way 8	K17	54
Atlantic Wk. 8	K17	54
Atlas St. 4	M9	23
Attercliffe Common 9	O8	24
Attercliffe Rd. 4 & 9	M9	23
Aubretia Av., Brin. 60	S8	26
Auckland Av. 6	G8	21
Auckland Dr. 19	T17	59
Auckland Ri. 19	T17	59
Auckland Way 19	T17	59
Audrey Rd. 13	P12	37
Aughton Clo. 13	P12	37
Aughton Cres. 13	P12	37
Aughton Dr. 13	P12	37
Aughton Rd., Aug. 31	V12	39
Augustus Rd., Brin. 60	S7	26
Aukley Rd. 8	K13	44
Austin Clo. 6	G8	21
Austin Ct. 6	G7	21
Avenue Rd. 7	K13	44
Avenue, The 9	P10	37
Catcliffe Rd.		
Avenue, The, Btn. 19	T14	49
Avenue, The, Dron. 18	L18	55
Avill Way, Wick. 66	X6	19
Avisford Dr. 5	J6	12
Avisford Rd. 5	J6	12
Avon Clo., C.A. 18	L18	55
Avondale Rd. 6	H8	21
Avondale Rd., Roth. 61	R4	6
Aylesbury Cres. 9	O6	14
Aylward Clo. 2	N12	36
Aylward Rd. 2	N12	36
Aysgarth Rd. 6	J5	12
Aysgarth Ri., Aug. 31	U12	39
Babington Clo. 2	N12	36
Babur Rd. 4	M9	23
Back La. 10	G10	33
Back La., Eck. 31	R18	58
Back La., Hoot.R. 65	Y1	9
Back La., Nether Haugh 62	S1	6
Back La., Thry. 65	W2	8
Backfields 1	L10	35
Division St.		
Backmoor Cres. 8	M15	45
Backmoor Rd. 8	M15	45

Bacon La. 9	N9	24
Baden St., Roth. 60	S4	16
Badger Clo. 13	S12	38
Badger Dr. 13	S12	38
Badger Pl. 13	S12	38
Badger Rd. 13	S12	38
Badger Ri. 13	S12	38
Badsley Ct., Roth. 65	T5	17
Badsley Moor La., Roth. 65	T5	17
Badsley St. S., Roth. 65	T5	17
Badsley St., Roth. 65	T5	17
Bagley Rd. 4	M7	23
Bagshaws Rd. 12	O13	46
Bagshot St. 11	J12	34
Bailey La. 1	K10	34
Bailey St. 1	L10	35
Baker St. 9	N9	24
Bakers Hill 1	L10	35
Fitzalan Sq.		
Bakers La. 1	K10	34
Solly St.		
Balaclava La. 6	K9	22
Balaclava Rd.		
Balaclava Rd. 6	K9	22
Baldwin St. 9	N9	24
Balfour Rd. 9	O9	24
Balk La., Bram. 66	Y5	19
Balk La., Brin. 60	R7	26
Balk, The, Roth. 61	R2	6
Ball Rd. 6	H8	21
Ball St. 3	K9	22
Ballifield Av. 13	R11	38
Ballifield Clo. 13	R11	38
Ballifield Cres. 13	R11	38
Ballifield Dr. 13	R11	38
Ballifield Pl. 13	R11	38
Ballifield Rd. 13	R11	38
Ballifield Ri. 13	R11	38
Ballifield Way 13	R11	38
Balm Grn. 1	L10	35
Balmain Dr. 6	H7	21
Balmain Rd. 6	H7	21
Balmoral Rd. 13	S13	48
Balmoral Way, Bram. 66	Y5	19
Baltic La. 9	M9	23
Attercliffe Rd.		
Baltic Rd. 9	N9	24
Baltic Way 9	N9	24
Baltic Rd.		
Bamforth St. 6	J8	22
Bank Clo. 7	K13	44
Bank Clo., Roth. 61	Q3	5
Bank St. 1	L10	35
Bank Ter. 10	J10	34
Parkers La.		
Bank Top Rd., Roth. 65	V6	18
Bankfield La., Stan. 6	F9	20
Bankfield Rd. 6	H8	21
Bankhouse Rd. 6	J9	22
Bankwood Clo. 14	M13	45
Bankwood Rd. 14	M13	45
Banner Cross Dr. 11	H13	43
Banner Cross Rd. 11	H13	43
Banner Ct. 11	H13	43
Bannerdale Clo. 11	J13	44
Bannerdale Rd. 7	J13	44
Bannerdale Vw. 11	J13	44
Bannham Rd. 9	P10	37
Bannon St. 6	J10	34
Barber Balk Clo., Roth. 61	Q3	5
Barber Balk Rd. 61	Q4	15
Barber Cres. 10	J10	34
Barber Pl. 10	J10	34
Barber Rd. 10	J10	34
Barber Wood Rd., Roth. 61	O4	14
Barbers Av., Raw. 62	T1	7
Barbers Cres., Raw. 62	T1	7
Barbot Hill Rd., Roth. 61	S3	6
Bard St.		
Bard St. 2	M10	35

Barden Cres., Brin. 60	S8	26
Bardwell Rd. 3	K9	22
Barfield Av., Whis. 60	U7	27
Barholm Rd. 10	G11	33
Baring Rd., Roth. 61	O5	14
Barkby Rd. 9	O6	14
Barkers Gro., Roth. 61	Q2	5
Barkers Pl. 6	J7	22
Parkside Rd.		
Barkers Pool 1	L10	35
Barkers Rd. 7	J13	44
Barlby Gro. 12	S14	48
Barley Wood Rd. 9	P9	25
Barlow Dr. 6	G9	21
Barlow Rd. 6	H8	21
Barmouth Rd. 7	K13	44
Barnard Av., C.A. 18	M18	55
Barnardiston Rd. 9	O9	24
Barncliffe Clo. 10	F11	32
Barncliffe Cres. 10	E11	32
Barncliffe Dr. 10	E11	32
Barncliffe Glen 10	E12	32
Barncliffe Rd. 10	E11	32
Barnes Av., D.Wd. 18	J18	54
Barnes Ct. 1	L11	35
Barnes La., D.Wd. 18	J18	54
Barnet Av. 11	G13	43
Barnet Rd. 11	G13	43
Barnfield Av. 10	G10	33
Barnfield Clo. 10	G10	33
Barnfield Dr. 10	G10	33
Barnfield Rd. 10	G10	33
Barnsdale Av. 19	R15	48
Barnsdale Av., Hack. 12	R15	48
Barnsley Rd. 4 & 5	M5	13
Barnsley Rd., Th.Hes. 61	N1	4
Baron St. 1	L11	35
Barrack La. 6	K9	22
Barretta St. 4	M7	23
Barrie Cres. 5	K6	12
Barrie Dr. 5	K6	12
Barrie Rd. 5	K6	12
Barrow Rd. 9	O6	14
Barrowby Rd., Roth. 60	U6	17
Bartle Av. 12	N14	46
Bartle Dr. 12	N14	46
Bartle Rd. 12	N14	46
Bartle Way 12	N14	46
Bartlett Clo. 6	F9	20
Bartlett Rd. 5	K6	12
Barton Rd. 8	L13	45
Basegreen Av. 12	O14	46
Basegreen Clo. 12	O14	46
Basegreen Cres. 12	O14	46
Basegreen Dr. 12	O14	46
Basegreen Pl. 12	O14	46
Basegreen Rd. 12	O14	46
Basegreen Way 12	P14	47
Basford Clo. 9	P9	25
Basford Dr. 9	O9	24
Basford Pl. 9	O9	24
Basford Pl. 9	P9	25
Basford St. 9	O9	24
Baslow Rd. 17	E18	52
Bassett La. 11	D13	41
Bassett Pl. 2	M11	35
Bassett Rd. 2	N11	36
Bassingthorpe La., Roth. 61	R3	6
Bassledene Rd. 2	O12	36
Bastock Rd. 6	J7	22
Batemoor Clo. 8	L17	55
Batemoor Dr. 8	L17	55
Batemoor Pl. 8	L17	55
Batemoor Rd. 8	L17	55
Batemoor Wk. 8	L17	55
Bates St. 10	J9	22
Batt St. 8	L12	35
Batworth Dr. 5	L8	23
Batworth Rd. 5	L8	23
Bawtry Gate 9	Q7	25
Bawtry Rd. 9	Q7	25
Bawtry Rd., Bram. 66	Y6	19
Bawtry Rd., Brin. 60	R7	26

Baxter Clo. 6	J 6	12
Baxter Dr. 6	J 6	12
Baxter Rd. 6	J 6	12
Baysdale Cft. 19	S16	58
Baytree Av., Bram. 66	Y 5	19
Bazley Rd. 2	N12	36
Beacon Clo. 4	N 7	24
Beacon Croft 4	N 7	24
Beacon Rd. 4	N 7	24
Beacon Way 4	N 7	24
Beaconsfield Rd.,	U 6	17
Roth. 60		
Bear Tree Rd. 62	T 2	7
Bear Tree St. 62	T 2	7
Beauchamp Rd., Roth. 61	Q 3	5
Beauchief Abbey La. 8	J16	54
Beauchief Dr. 17	J16	54
Beauchief Ri. 8	J15	44
Beaufort Rd. 10	J10	34
Beaumont Av. 2	O11	36
Beaumont Clo. 2	O11	36
Beaumont Cres. 2	O11	36
Beaumont Dr., Roth. 65	U 5	17
Beaumont Rd. N. 2	O11	36
Beaumont Way 2	O11	36
Beaver Av. 13	R12	38
Beaver Clo. 13	R12	38
Beaver Dr. 13	R12	38
Beaver Hill Rd. 13	R12	38
Beck Clo. 5	N 4	14
Beck Rd. 5	M 4	13
Becket Av. 8	J17	54
Becket Cres. 8	K17	54
Becket Rd. 8	K17	54
Becket Wk. 8	J17	54
Beckett Cres., Roth. 61	P 3	5
Beckford La. 5	M 4	13
Beckton Av. 19	T15	49
Beckton Ct. 19	T15	49
Beckwith Rd., Roth. 65	V 4	18
Bedale Rd. 8	K13	44
Bedford Rd., Ought. 30	F 4	10
Bedford St. 6	K 9	22
Bee St. 9	O 8	24
Beech Av., Raw. 62	U 1	7
Beech Av., Roth. 65	W 6	18
Beech Gro., Bram. 66	Y 5	19
Beech Hill Rd. 10	J11	34
Beech Way, Aug. 31	U12	39
Beeches Av. 2	M12	35
Beeches Dr. 2	M12	35
Beeches Gro. 19	U14	49
Beeches Gro., Btn. 19	U14	49
Beechwood Clo.,	U 1	7
Raw. 62		
Beechwood Rd. 6	H 8	21
Beechwood Rd., Roth. 60	U 6	17
Beehive Rd. 10	J10	34
Beeley St. 2	K11	34
London Rd.		
Beeley Wood La. 6	H 6	11
Beeley Wood Rd. 6	J 6	12
Beely Rd., Ought. 30	G 5	11
Beet St. 3	K10	34
Beeton Rd. 8	K13	44
Beevers Rd., Roth. 61	P 3	5
Beighton Rd. 12 & 19	R14	48
Beighton Rd., Wood. 13	S13	48
Beighton Road E. 19	S14	48
Belcourt Rd., Roth. 65	V 6	18
Beldon Clo. 2	M12	35
Beldon Pl. 2	M12	35
Beldon Rd. 2	M12	35
Belgrave Dr. 10	F11	32
Belgrave Rd. 10	G11	33
Belgrave Sq. 2	L12	35
Bell Hagg Rd. 6	H 9	21
Bellefield St. 3	K10	34
Bellhouse Rd. 5	M 6	13
Bellhouse Ter. 5	M 6	13
Bellhouse Rd.		
Bellows Rd., Raw. 62	T 1	7
Bells Sq. 1	L10	35
Pinfold St.		

Bellscroft Av.,	W 3	8
Thry. 65		
Belmont St., Roth. 61	R 5	16
Belmonte Gdns. 2	M11	35
Belmoor Rd. 9	O 8	24
Belper Rd. 7	K13	44
Belsize Rd. 10	G12	33
Belvedere Clo.,	Y 4	19
Bram. 66		
Belvedere Par.,	Y 5	19
Bram. 66		
Ben Clo. 6	G 7	21
Ben La. 6	G 7	21
Bennett Clo., Raw. 62	U 1	7
Bennett St. 2	K12	34
Bennett St., Roth. 61	Q 5	15
Benson Rd. 2	N11	36
Bent Lathes Ave.,	V 6	18
Roth. 60		
Bentfield Av., Roth. 60	V 6	18
Bentley Rd. 6	H 9	21
Bentley St., Roth. 60	S 6	16
Benton Ct., Roth. 61	Q 4	15
Benton Way, Roth. 61	Q 4	15
Bents Clo. 11	G13	43
Bents Cres. 11	G13	43
Bents Cres., C.A. 18	M18	55
Bents Dr. 11	G13	43
Bents Green Av. 11	G13	43
Bents Green Pl. 11	G13	43
Bents Green Rd. 11	G13	43
Bents La., C.A. 18	M18	55
Bents Rd. 11	G13	43
Bents Rd., Roth. 61	Q 3	5
Bents Rd., Tot. 17	F18	52
Benty La. 10	G10	33
Beresford Rd. 11	J12	34
Stewart Rd.		
Berkley Rd. 9	O 8	24
Bernard Rd. 2	M10	35
Bernard St. 2	M10	35
Bernard St., Raw. 62	U 1	7
Bernard St., Roth. 60	T 5	17
Berners Clo. 2	N13	46
Berners Dr. 2	N13	46
Berners Pl. 2	N13	46
Berners Rd. 2	N13	46
Bernshall Cres. 5	L 4	13
Berry Av., Eck. 31	S18	58
Bertha St., Roth. 60	S 4	16
Bertram Rd., Ought. 30	G 5	11
Bessemer Pl. 9	N 9	24
Stevenson Rd.		
Bessemer Rd. 9	N 9	24
Bessingby Rd. 6	J 8	22
Bethel Rd., Roth. 65	T 4	17
Bethel Wk. 1	L10	35
Cambridge St.		
Beulah Rd. 6	J 7	22
Bevercotes Rd. 5	M 6	13
Beverle` St. 9	O 9	24
Beverleys Rd. 8	L14	45
Bevin Pl., Raw. 62	U 1	7
Bevis Row 2	M10	35
Hyde Pk.		
Bickerton Rd. 6	J 7	22
Bigby Way, Rav. 65	Y 4	19
Bignor Pl. 12	J 5	12
Lyminster Rd.		
Bignor Rd. 6	J 5	12
Lyminster Rd.		
Billam Pl., Roth. 61	Q 3	5
Billam St., Eck. 31	R18	58
Bilston St. 6	J 8	22
Burton St.		
Bilton Rd. 9	O 9	24
Binders Rd., Roth. 61	Q 3	5
Binfield Rd. 8	K13	44
Bingham Park Cres. 11	H12	33
Bingham Park Rd. 11	H12	33
Bingham Pl. 8	K15	44
Woodseats House Rd.		
Bingham Rd. 8	K15	44
Bingley La. 6	E10	32

Binsted Av. 5	J 6	12
Binsted Clo. 5	J 6	12
Binsted Cres. 5	J 6	12
Binsted Croft 5	J 6	12
Binsted Dr. 5	J 6	12
Binsted Gdns. 5	J 6	12
Binsted Glade 5	J 6	12
Binsted Gro. 5	J 6	12
Binsted Rd. 5	J 6	12
Binsted Way 5	J 6	12
Birch Cres., Wick. 66	Y 5	19
Birch Farm Av. 8	L16	55
Birch Gro., Ought. 30	F 5	10
Birch House Av.,	F 5	10
Ought. 30		
Birch Pl. 9	N 9	24
Birch Rd.		
Birch Rd. 9	N 9	24
Birchall Av., Whis. 60	U 7	27
Birches Fold, C.A. 18	M18	55
Birchitt Clo. 17	J17	54
Birchitt Pl. 17	J17	54
Birchitt Rd. 17	J17	54
Birchitt Vw., Dron. 18	L18	55
Birchtree Rd.,	N 2	4
Th.Hes. 61		
Birchvale Rd. 12	P14	47
Birchwood Av., Raw. 62	T 1	7
Birchwood Clo.,	T16	59
Mosb. 19		
Birchwood Croft,	T16	59
Mosb. 19		
Birchwood Dr., Rav. 65	Y 4	19
Birchwood Gdns.,	T16	59
Mosb. 19		
Birchwood Gro.,	T16	59
Mosb. 19		
Birchwood Rd.,	P18	57
Marsh. 31		
Birchwood Ri., Mosb. 19	T16	59
Birchwood Vw., Mosb. 19	T16	59
Birchwood Way, Mosb. 19	T16	59
Birdwell Rd. 4	N 7	24
Birkendale 6	J 9	22
Birkendale Rd. 6	J 9	22
Birkendale Vw. 6	J 9	22
Birklands Av. 13	Q11	37
Birklands Clo. 13	Q11	37
Birklands Dr. 13	Q11	37
Birks Av. 13	R13	48
Birks Rd., Roth. 61	Q 3	5
Birks Wood Dr.,	F 5	10
Ought. 30		
Birley La. 12	P15	47
Birley Moor Av. 12	Q14	47
Birley Moor Clo. 12	Q14	47
Birley Moor Cres. 12·	Q14	47
Birley Moor Dr. 12	Q15	47
Birley Moor Pl. 12	Q15	47
Birley Moor Rd. 12	P13	47
Birley Moor Way 12	Q15	47
Birley Rise Cres. 6	J 6	12
Birley Rise Rd. 6	J 6	12
Birley Spa La. 12	Q14	47
Birley Spa Wk. 12	R14	48
Carter Lodge Av.		
Birley Vale Av. 12	P13	47
Birley Vale Clo. 12	P13	47
Birley Vw., Wor. 30	F 5	10
Bisby Rd., Raw. 62	U 1	7
Bishop Hill 13	R13	48
Bishop St. 3	K11	34
Bishops Clo. 8	L13	45
Bishopscourt Rd. 8	L13	45
Bishopsholme Clo. 5	L 7	23
Bishopsholme Rd. 5	L 7	23
Bittern Vw., Th.Hes. 61	O 1	4
Black Carr Rd.,	X 5	19
Wick. 66		
Black Hill Rd.,	V 6	18
Roth. 65		
Black La., Lox. 6	F 8	20
Black Swan Wk. 1	L10	35
Fargate		

82

Blackamoor Cres. 17 — F17 52
Blackamoor Rd. 17 — F17 52
Blackamoor Vw. 17 — F17 52
Blackberry Flats, Mosb. 19 — T16 59
Blackbrook Av. 10 — E11 32
Blackbrook Dr. 10 — E11 32
Blackbrook Rd. 10 — E11 32
Blackburn Rd., Roth. 61 — O5 14
Blackburne St. 6 — J8 22
Burton St.
Blackdown Av. 19 — S15 48
Blackdown Clo. 19 — S15 48
Blackmore Cres., Brin. 60 — R7 26
Blackmore St. 4 — M9 23
Blacksmith La., Gren. 30 — J4 12
Blackstock Clo. 14 — M15 45
Blackstock Cres. 14 — M15 45
Blackstock Dr. 14 — M15 45
Blackstock Rd. 8 — M15 45
Blackthorn Av., Bram. 66 — Y5 19
Blaco Rd. 9 — O8 24
Blagden St. 2 — M10 35
Blair Athol Rd. 11 — H13 43
Blake Clo., Bram. 66 — Y6 19
Blake St. 6 — J9 22
Blakegrove Rd. 6 — K9 22
Upperthorpe
Blakeney Rd. 10 — J10 34
Bland La. 6 — G7 21
Bland St. 4 — N8 24
Blast La. 2 — M10 35
Blaxton Clo. 19 — R15 48
Blaxton Clo., Hack. 19 — R15 48
Blayton Rd. 4 — M8 23
Blenheim Clo., Bram. 66 — Y4 19
Blenheim Ct., Bram. 66 — X5 19
Blonk St. 1 — L10 35
Blossom Cres. 19 — O14 46
Blue Boy St. 3 — K10 34
Bluebell Rd. 5 — N6 14
Blyde Rd. 5 — M7 23
Blyth Av., Raw. 62 — T1 7
Blyth Clo., Whis. 60 — V7 28
Bochum Park Way 8 — L16 55
Bocking La. 8 — J15 44
Bocking Ri. 8 — K16 54
Boden Pl. 9 — P9 25
Bodmin St. 9 — N9 24
Boggard La., Ought. 30 — F5 10
Boiley La., Killa. 31 — U18 59
Boland Rd. 8 — J17 54
Bold St. 9 — O8 24
Bole Hill La. 10 — H10 33
Bole Hill Rd. 6 — H9 21
Bole Hill, Tree. 60 — T9 27
Bolsover Rd. 5 — M7 23
Bolsover Rd. E. 5 — M7 23
Firth Park Rd.
Bolsover St. 3 — K10 34
Bolton St. 3 — K11 34
Bonet La., Brin. 60 — R7 26
Bonville Gdns. 3 — K10 34
Dover St.
Booker Rd. 8 — K15 44
Booth Clo. 19 — S15 48
Booth Croft 19 — S15 48
Booth Rd., Roth. 61 — R2 6
Bootle St. 9 — O9 24
Worksop Rd.
Borough Rd. 6 — J8 22
Borrowdale Av. 19 — T17 59
Borrowdale Clo. 19 — T17 59
Borrowdale Dr. 19 — T17 59
Borrowdale Rd. 19 — T17 59
Boston Castle Gro., Roth. 60 — T6 17
Boston St. 2 — K11 34
Bosville Clo., Rav. 65 — Y2 9
Bosville Rd. 10 — H10 33
Lydgate La.

Bosville St., Roth. 65 — V4 18
Boswell St., Roth. 65 — T5 17
Bosworth St. 10 — H10 33
Newent La.
Botanical Rd. 11 — J11 34
Botham St. 4 — N8 24
Botham St. N. 4 — N8 24
Botsford St. 3 — L9 23
Boundary Grn., Raw. 62 — T2 7
Boundary Rd. 2 — N11 36
Bourne Rd. 5 — M6 13
Bowden Wood Av. 9 — P11 37
Bowden Wood Clo. 9 — P11 37
Bowden Wood Cres. 9 — P11 37
Bowden Wood Dr. 9 — P11 37
Bowden Wood Pl. 9 — P11 37
Bowden Wood Rd. 9 — P11 37
Bowdon St. 1 — K11 34
Bowen Dr., Thry. 65 — W3 8
Bowen Rd., Roth. 65 — T4 17
Bower Clo., Roth. 61 — Q3 5
Bower La., Gren. 30 — H4 11
Bower Rd. 10 — J10 34
Bower Spring 3 — L10 35
Bower St. 3 — L10 35
Bowfield Rd. 5 — M6 13
Bowling Green St. 3 — L9 23
Bowman Clo. 12 — N15 46
Bowman Dr. 12 — N15 46
Bowness Rd. 6 — J8 22
Bowood Rd. 11 — J12 34
Bowshaw Av. 8 — L17 55
Bowshaw Clo. 8 — L17 55
Bowshaw Cotts., Dron. 18 — L17 55
Bowshaw Vw. 8 — L17 55
Boyce St. 6 — J9 22
Boyland St. 3 — K9 22
Boynton Cres. 5 — L7 23
Boynton Rd. 5 — K7 22
Bracken Ct., Wick. 66 — X6 19
Bracken Rd. 5 — N6 14
Brackenfield Gro. 12 — P14 47
Brackley St. 3 — L9 23
Bradbury St. 8 — L13 45
Bradfield Rd. 6 — J8 22
Bradgate Clo., Roth. 61 — R4 16
Bradgate Croft, Roth. 61 — R4 16
Bradgate Ct., Roth. 61 — Q4 15
Bradgate La., Roth. 61 — Q4 15
Bradgate Pl., Roth. 61 — R4 16
Bradgate Rd., Roth. 61 — R4 16
Bradley Ri., Raw. 62 — U1 7
Bradley St. 10 — H9 21
Bradstone Rd., Roth. 65 — V4 18
Bradway Clo. 17 — H17 53
Bradway Dr. 17 — H17 53
Bradway Grange Rd. 17 — J17 54
Bradway Rd. 17 — H17 53
Bradwell St. 2 — L12 35
Braemore Rd. 6 — H7 21
Brailsford Av. 5 — L4 13
Brailsford Rd. 5 — L4 13
Braithwell Rd., Rav. 65 — Y4 19
Bramall La. 2 — L11 35
Bramble Clo., Wick. 66 — X6 19
Brameld Rd., Raw. 62 — T1 7
Bramham Rd. 9 — O9 24
Bramley Av. 13 — Q12 37
Bramley Clo. 19 — S16 58
Bramley Dr. 13 — Q11 37
Bramley Hall Rd. 13 — Q12 37
Bramley La. 13 — Q11 37
Bramley Park Rd. 13 — Q11 37
Brampton Av., Thur. 66 — Y9 29
Brampton Clo., Thur. 66 — Y9 29
Brampton Ct., Hack. 12 — R15 48
Brampton La., Bram.M. 31 — X9 29
Brampton Rd., Thur. 66 — Y9 29
Bramshill Clo. 19 — U15 49
Bramshill Ct. 19 — U15 49

Bramwell Gdns. 3 — K10 34
Weston St.
Bramwell St. 3 — K10 34
Bramwell St., Roth. 65 — T4 17
Bramwith Rd. 11 — G12 33
Brandon St. 3 — L8 23
Brandreth Clo. 6 — K9 22
Brandreth Rd. 6 — K9 22
Upperthorpe
Bransby St. 6 — J9 22
Brathay Clo. 4 — N7 24
Brathay Rd. 4 — N7 24
Bray St. 9 — O9 24
Bray Wk., Roth. 61 — P3 5
Brecklands, Roth. 60 — V6 18
Brecklands, Wick. 66 — X6 19
Brecks Cres., Roth. 65 — W6 18
Brecks La., Roth. 65 — V5 18
Brecon Clo., Btn. 19 — U15 49
Brentwood Av. 11 — J13 44
Brentwood Rd. 11 — J13 44
Bressingham Clo. 4 — M9 23
Bressingham Rd. 4 — L9 23
Bretton Gro. 12 — P14 47
Briar Rd. 7 — K13 44
Briarfield Av. 12 — O14 46
Briarfield Cres. 12 — O14 46
Briarfield Rd. 12 — O14 46
Briarfields La., Wor. 30 — F5 10
Brick St. 10 — H10 33
Brickhouse La. 17 — F16 52
Bridby St. 13 — S13 48
Bridge Hill 30 — F4 10
Langsett Rd. N.
Bridge St. 3 — L9 23
Bridge St., Roth. 60 — S4 16
Bridgegate, Roth. 60 — S5 16
Bridgehouses 3 — L9 23
Nursery St.
Bridle La., Marsh. 31 — O18 56
Bridle Stile 19 — S16 58
Bridle Stile Av. 19 — R16 58
Bridle Stile Clo. 19 — S16 58
Bridleway, The, Raw. 62 — V1 7
Bridport Rd. 9 — O9 24
Brier Clo. 19 — S15 48
Brier St. 6 — J8 22
Brierley Rd., Dalton 65 — W3 8
Briery Wk., Roth. 61 — R2 6
Bright St. 9 — O8 24
Brightmore Dr. 3 — K10 34
Mitchell St.
Brighton Terrace Rd. 10 — J10 34
Brightside La. 9 — O7 24
Brimmesfield Clo. 2 — N12 36
Brimmesfield Dr. 2 — N12 36
Brimmesfield Rd. 2 — N12 36
Brincliffe Cres. 11 — J12 34
Brincliffe Edge Clo. 11 — J13 44
Brincliffe Edge Rd. 11 — H13 43
Brincliffe Gdns. 11 — J12 34
Brincliffe Hill 11 — H12 33
Brindley Clo. 8 — L14 45
Brindley Cres. 8 — L14 45
Brinkburn Clo. 17 — G17 53
Brinkburn Dr. 17 — G17 53
Brinkburn Vale Rd. 17 — G17 53
Brinsford Rd., Brin. 60 — S7 26
Brinsworth Hall Av., Brin. 60 — R8 26
Brinsworth Hall Cres., Brin. 60 — R8 26
Brinsworth Hall Dr., Brin. 60 — R8 26
Brinsworth Hall Gro., Brin. 60 — R8 26
Brinsworth La., Brin. 60 — R8 26
Brinsworth Rd., Brin. 60 — R8 26
Brinsworth St. 9 — N9 24
Bristol Rd. 11 — J11 34

Street	Grid	
Carnarvon St. 6	K 9	22
Carpenter Cft. 12	P13	47
Carpenter Gdns. 12	P13	47
Carpenter Ms. 12	P13	47
Carr Bank Clo. 10	G12	33
Carr Bank Dr. 11	G12	33
Carr Bank La. 11	G12	33
Carr Forge Clo. 12	R14	48
Carr Forge La. 12	R14	48
Carr Forge Mt. 12	R14	48
Carr Forge Pl. 12	R14	48
Carr Forge Rd. 12	R14	48
Carr Forge Ter. 12	R14	48
Carr Forge Vw. 12	R14	48
Carr Forge Wk. 12	R14	48
Carter Lodge Av.		
Carr La. 1	K10	34
Carr La., Roth. 65	X 1	9
Carr Rd. 6	J 9	22
Carrfield Ct. 8	L13	45
Carrfield St.		
Carrfield Dr. 8	L13	45
Carrfield La. 2	L13	45
Carrfield Rd. 8	L13	45
Carrfield St. 8	L13	45
Carrill Dr. 6	J 5	12
Carrill Rd. 6	J 5	12
Carrington Rd. 11	H12	33
Carrington St., Roth. 65	T 5	17
Carrville Dr. 6	J 6	12
Carrville Rd. 6	J 6	12
Carrville Rd. W. 6	J 6	12
Carrwell La. 6	J 6	12
Carsick Gro. 10	F11	32
Tom La.		
Carsick Hill Cres. 10	F11	32
Carsick Hill Dr. 10	F11	32
Carsick Hill Cres.		
Carsick Hill Rd. 10	F11	32
Carsick Hill Way 10	F11	32
Carsick View Rd. 10	F11	32
Carson Mt. 12	O14	46
Carson Rd. 10	H10	33
Carter Knowle Av. 11	J13	44
Carter Knowle Rd. 7 & 11	H13	43
Carter Lodge Av. 12	R14	48
Carter Lodge Dr. 12	R14	48
Carter Lodge Pl. 12	R14	48
Carter Lodge Ri. 12	R14	48
Carter Lodge Wk. 12	R14	48
Carter Rd. 8	L13	45
Carterhall La. 12	O15	46
Carterhall Rd. 12	O15	46
Carters Yd., Btn. 19	U14	49
High St.		
Cartmell Cres. 8	K14	44
Cartmell Rd. 8	K14	44
Carvale Dr. 13	P12	37
Carvale Vw. 13	P12	37
Carver La. 1	L10	35
Carver St. 1	L10	35
Carwood Clo. 4	M 8	23
Carwood Grn. 4	M 8	23
Carwood Gro. 4	M 8	23
Carwood La. 4	M 8	23
Carwood Rd. 4	M 8	23
Carwood Way 4	M 8	23
Cary Rd. 2	N12	36
Cary Rd., Eck. 31	R18	58
Castle Av., Roth. 60	S 6	16
Castle Grn. 3	L10	35
Castle Hill, Eck. 31	S18	58
Castle Sq. 1	L10	35
Castle St. 3	L10	35
Castlebeck Av. 2	O11	36
Castlebeck Cft. 2	P11	37
Castlebeck Ct. 2	P11	37
Castlebeck Av.		
Castledine Cft. 9	O 7	24
Castledine Gdns. 9	O 7	24
Castlefolds 1	L10	35
Exchange St.		
Castlegate 1	L10	35
Castlerow Clo. 17	H17	53
Castlerow Dr. 17	H17	53
Castlewood Cres. 10	E12	32
Castlewood Dr. 10	E12	32
Castlewood Rd. 10	E12	32
Castor Rd. 9	N 8	24
Cat La. 2	M13	45
Catch Bar La. 6	J 7	22
Catcliffe Rd. 9	P10	37
Catherine Rd. 4	L 9	23
Catherine St. 3	L 9	23
Catherine St., Roth. 65	T 5	17
Catley Rd. 9	P 9	25
Cattal St. 9	O 9	24
Causeway Gdns. 17	F16	52
Causeway Glade 17	F16	52
Causeway Head Rd. 17	F16	52
Causeway, The 17	F16	52
Cave St. 9	N 9	24
Cavendish Av. 17	G16	53
Cavendish Av. 6	G 7	21
Cavendish Clo., Roth. 65	V 6	18
Cavendish Rd. 11	J12	34
Cavendish Rd., Roth. 61	R 5	16
Cavendish St. 3	K10	34
Cavill Rd. 8	L14	45
Cawdor Rd. 2	N13	46
Cawdron Ri., Brin. 60	S 8	26
Cawston Rd. 4	M 8	23
Cawthorne Clo. 8	K14	44
Cawthorne Clo., Roth. 65	V 4	18
Cawthorne Gro. 8	K14	44
Cawthorne Rd., Roth. 65	V 4	18
Caxton La. 10	H11	33
Caxton Rd. 10	J11	34
Cecil Av., Dron. 18	L18	55
Cecil Rd. 7	K12	34
Cecil Rd., Dron. 18	L18	55
Cecil Sq. 2	K12	34
Cedar Av., Wick. 66	Y 5	19
Celandine Gdns. 17	H17	53
Cemetery Av. 11	J11	34
Cemetery Rd. 11	K12	34
Centenary Way, Roth. 60	S 6	16
Central Av., Bram. 66	X 4	19
Central Av., Roth. 65	U 4	17
Central Dr., Thur. 66	Y 9	29
Central Rd., Roth. 65	S 5	16
Centre, The, Bram. 66	Y 5	19
Century St. 9	O 9	24
Chadwick Rd. 13	P12	37
Chaff La., Whis. 60	U 7	27
Chaffinch Av., Brin. 60	S 8	26
Challoner Grn., Mosb. 19	T16	59
Challoner Way, Mosb. 19	T16	59
Chambers La. 4	N 7	24
Chambers Rd., Roth. 61	Q 3	5
Champion Clo. 5	M 5	13
Champion Rd. 5	M 5	13
Chancet Wood Clo. 8	K16	54
Chancet Wood Dr. 8	K16	54
Chancet Wood Rd. 8	K15	44
Chancet Wood Ri. 8	K16	54
Chancet Wood Vw. 8	K16	54
Chandos St. 10	J11	34
Nile St.		
Channing Gdns. 6	J 8	22
Langsett Cres.		
Chantrey Rd. 8	K14	44
Chantry Bridge, Roth. 60	S 4	16
Chapel Clo. 10	G11	33
Chapel Clo., Roth. 61	R 2	6
Chapel Hills, Whis. 60	U 7	27
Chapel La., Totley 17	F18	52
Chapel La. 9	O 9	24
Worksop Rd.		
Chapel Rd. 9	O 9	24
Chapel Rd., Mosb. 19	S17	58
Chapel St., Raw. 62	T 1	7
Chapel St., Roth. 61	R 2	6
Chapel St., Wood. 13	R13	48
Chapel Ter. 10	G11	33
Chapel Wk. 1	L10	35
Chapel Wk., Roth. 60	S 5	16
Chapelfield Cres., Th.Hes. 61	N 1	4
Chapelfield Dr., Th.Hes. 61	N 1	4
Chapelfield Mt., Th.Hes. 61	N 1	4
Chapelfield Pl., Th.Hes. 61	N 1	4
Chapelfield Rd., Th.Hes. 61	N 1	4
Chapelfield Way, Th.Hes. 61	N 1	4
Chapelwood Rd. 9	O 9	25
Chapman St. 9	O 6	14
Charles Ashmore Rd. 8	K16	54
Charles La. 1	L10	24
Norfolk St.		
Charles St. 1	L10	35
Charles St., Kiln. 62	W 1	8
Charles St., Raw. 62	U 1	7
Charles St., Roth. 60	S 4	16
Charlotte La. 1	K10	34
Mappin St.		
Charlotte Rd. 1 & 2	L11	35
Charnley Av. 11	J13	44
Charnley Clo. 11	J13	44
Charnley Dr. 11	J13	44
Charnley Ri. 11	J13	44
Charnock Av. 12	O15	46
Charnock Cres. 12	O14	46
Charnock Dale Rd. 12	O15	46
Charnock Dr. 12	O15	46
Charnock Gro. 12	O15	46
Charnock Hall Rd. 12	O15	46
Charnock View Rd. 12	O15	46
Charnock Wood Rd. 12	O15	46
Charnwood Ct., Btn. 19	U15	49
Charnwood Gro., Roth. 60	Q 4	15
Charter Row 1	K11	34
Charter Sq. 1	L11	35
Chase Rd., Lox. 6	F 7	20
Chatfield Rd. 8	K15	44
Chatham St. 3	L 9	23
Chatham St., Roth. 65	T 5	17
Chatsworth Park Av. 12	O13	46
Chatsworth Park Dr. 12	O13	46
Chatsworth Park Gro. 12	O13	46
Chatsworth Park Rd. 12	O13	46
Chatsworth Park Ri. 12	O13	46
Chatsworth Rd., Roth. 61	R 5	16
Chatsworth Rd., Tot. 17	G17	53
Chatsworth Ri., Brin. 60	S 8	26
Chatterton Dr., Roth. 65	U 6	17
Chatwin St. 6	J10	34
Horam Rd.		
Chaucer Clo. 5	J 5	12
Chaucer Rd. 5	K 5	12
Chaucer Rd., Roth. 65	U 6	17
Cheadle St. 6	J 8	22
Chelmsford St. 9	N 9	24
Chelsea Ct. 11	J12	34
Chelsea Rd. 11	J12	34
Chelsea Ri. 11	J12	34
Cheney Row 1	L10	35
Pinstone St.		
Cherry Bank Rd. 8	L14	45
Cherry St. 2	L12	35
Cherry St. S. 2	L12	35
Cherry Tree Clo. 11	J12	34
Cherry Tree Cres., Wick. 66	Y 5	19
Cherry Tree Dell 11	J12	34
Cherry Tree Dr. 7	J12	34
Cherry Tree Rd. 11	J12	34

Name	Ref		Name	Ref		Name	Ref
Cherrytree Clo.,	S 8 26		Clarke Dell 10	J11 34		Coates St. 2	M11 35
Brin. 60			Clarke Dr. 10	J11 34		Duke St.	
Chessel Clo. 8	L14 45		Clarke Sq. 2	K12 34		Cobden Pl. 10	J10 34
Chester La. 1	K10 34		Clarke St. 10	K11 34		Cobden View Rd.	
Chester St. 1	K10 34		Clarkegrove Rd. 10	J11 34		Cobden Ter. 10	J10 34
Chesterfield Rd. 8	K15 44		Clarkehouse Rd. 10	J11 34		Cobden View Rd.	
Chesterfield Rd. S. 8	L17 55		Clarkson St. 10	K10 34		Cobden View Ms. 10	H10 33
Chesterfield Rd.,	R18 58		Clay La. 1	L11 35		Cobden View Rd.	
Eck. 31			Eyre St.			Cobden View Rd. 10	H10 33
Chesterfield Rd.,	U13 49		Clay St. 9	N 8 24		Cobnar Av. 8	L15 45
Swall. 31			Clay Wheels La. 6	H 6 11		Cobnar Dr. 8	L15 45
Chesterhill Av.,	W 3 8		Claypit La., Raw. 62	U 1 7		Cobnar Gdns. 8	K15 44
Dal.M. 65			Clayton Cres., Btn. 19	T15 49		Bingham Rd.	
Chesterton Rd.,	U 3 7		Clayton Hollow 19	T15 49		Cobnar Rd. 8	K15 44
Roth. 65			Claywood Dr. 2	M11 35		Cockayne Pl. 8	K14 44
Chesterwood Dr. 10	H11 33		Claywood Rd. 2	M11 35		Cockshutt Av. 8	J16 54
Chestnut Av. 9	Q10 37		Cleeve Hill Gdns. 19	S15 48		Cockshutt Dr. 8	J16 54
Chestnut Av., Btn. 19	T13 49		Clematis Rd. 5	N 6 14		Cockshutt Rd. 8	J16 54
Chestnut Av., Roth. 65	U 4 17		Clement St. 9	O 9 24		Cockshutts La.,	F 4 10
Chestnut Clo., Bram. 66	X 5 19		Clement St., Roth. 61	Q 5 15		Ought. 30	
Chestnut Rd., Aug. 31	U12 39		Clementson Rd. 10	J10 34		Coisley Hill 13	Q13 47
Chevril Ct., Wick. 66	X 6 19		Clevedon St. 4	N 8 24		Coisley Rd. 13	R13 48
Chichester Rd. 10	H10 33		Petre St.			Coit La. 11	F14 42
Chiltern Rd. 6	H 8 21		Cleveland St. 6	K 9 22		Coke Hill, Roth. 60	S 5 16
Chiltern Ri., Brin. 60	S 8 26		Cliff Rd., Stan. 6	F 9 20		Coke La., Roth. 60	S 5 16
Chinley St. 9	O 9 24		Cliff St. 11	K11 34		Colby Pl. 6	G 9 21
Chippingham Pl. 9	N 9 24		Cliffe Farm Dr. 11	H12 33		Colchester Rd. 10	H10 33
Shortridge St.			Cliffe Field Rd. 8	K13 44		Mulehouse Rd.	
Chippingham St. 9	N 9 24		Cliffe House Rd. 5	L 6 13		Coldwell Hill,	E 4 10
Chippinghouse Rd. 7 & 8	K12 34		Cliffe Rd. 6	H 9 21		Ought. 30	
Chiverton Clo.,	L18 55		Cliffe View Rd. 8	L13 45		Coldwell La. 10	G10 33
Dron. 18			Cliffe Field Rd.			Coleford Rd. 9	P 9 25
Chorley Av. 10	F12 32		Clifford Av., Thry. 65	X 3 9		Coleman St. 62	T 2 7
Chorley Dr. 10	F12 32		Clifford Rd. 11	J12 34		Coleridge Gdns. 9	O 9 24
Chorley Pl. 10	F12 32		Clifford Rd., Roth. 61	Q 3 5		Stovin Dr.	
Chorley Rd. 10	F12 32		Clifton Av. 9	Q10 37		Coleridge Pl. 9	O 9 24
Christchurch Rd. 3	L 8 23		Clifton Av., Roth. 65	U 5 17		Coleridge Rd.	
Church Av., Raw. 62	T 2 7		Clifton Bank, Roth. 60	T 5 17		Coleridge Rd. 9	O 8 24
Church Clo. 30	F 4 10		Clifton Cres. 9	Q10 37		Coleridge Rd., Roth. 65	T 4 17
Church Fields, Roth. 61	Q 4 15		Clifton Cres. N.,	T 5 17		Colister Dr. 9	O10 36
Church La., Attercliffe 9	N 9 24		Roth. 65			Colister Gdns. 9	P10 37
Burgess Rd.			Clifton Gro., Roth. 65	T 5 17		College Clo. 4	M 8 23
Church La., Bram. 66	Y 5 19		Clifton La. 9	Q11 37		College Ct. 4	M 8 23
Church La., Dore 17	F17 52		Clifton La., Roth. 65	T 5 17		College Park Clo.,	T 6 17
Church La., Hack. 12	S14 48		Clifton Mt., Roth. 65	T 5 17		Roth. 60	
Church La., Rav. 65	Y 2 9		Clifton St. 9	O 8 24		College Rd., Roth. 60	S 5 16
Church La., Ridg. 12	P16 57		Clifton Ter., Roth. 65	T 5 17		College St. 10	J11 34
Church La., Tree. 60	T10 39		Clifton Vill.,	T 5 17		College St., Roth. 65	S 5 16
Church La., Wick. 66	X 6 19		Roth. 60			Collegiate Cres. 10	J11 34
Church La., Wood. 13	R13 48		Clinton La. 10	K11 34		Colley Av. 5	L 5 13
Church St. 1	L10 35		Clinton Pl. 10	K11 34		Colley Clo. 5	L 5 13
Church St., Eck. 31	T18 59		Clipstone Gdns. 9	P 9 25		Colley Cres. 5	L 5 13
Church St., Greas. 61	R 2 6		Clipstone Rd. 9	P 9 25		Colley Dr. 5	L 5 13
Church St., Kimb. 61	Q 4 15		Clixby Rd. 9	N 8 24		Colley Rd. 5	L 5 13
Church St., Ought. 30	F 4 10		Cloonmore Cft. 8	M15 45		Colliers Clo. 13	R13 48
Church St., Raw. 62	T 2 7		Cloonmore Dr. 8	M15 45		Colliery Rd. 8	O 7 24
Church St., Roth. 60	S 5 16		Clough Bank 2	L12 35		Collin Av. 6	H 7 21
Church St., Stan. 6	F 9 20		Clough Bank,	R 4 16		Collingbourne Av. 19	U15 49
Church View, Thry. 65	W 2 8		Roth. 61			Collingbourne Dr. 19	U15 49
Church Vw. 13	S12 38		Clough Fields 10	G10 33		Collinson Rd. 5	L 6 13
Churchdale Rd. 12	P14 47		Clough La. 10	E13 41		Colver Rd. 2	L12 35
Churchfield Dr.,	X 6 19		Clough Rd. 1 & 2	L11 35		Colwall St. 9	N 9 24
Wick. 66			Clough Rd., Roth. 61	R 4 16		Commercial St. 1	L10 35
Churchill Rd. 10	J10 34		Clough St., Roth. 61	R 4 16		Common La. 11	F13 42
Cinder Hill La.,	J 4 12		Clough Wood Vw.,	F 4 10		Common La., Thur. 66	Y 9 29
Gren. 30			Ought. 30			Common Side 10	J10 34
Cinderbridge Rd.,	S 2 6		Clover Grn., Roth. 61	Q 3 5		Compton St. 6	H 9 21
Roth. 61			Club Garden Rd. 11	K12 34		Conalan Av. 17	H17 53
Cinderhill La. 8	L16 55		Club Garden Wk. 11	K11 34		Concord Rd. 5	N 5 14
Cinderhill Rd.,	Q 3 5		Club Garden Rd.			Concord View Rd.,	P 5 15
Roth. 61			Club Mill Rd. 6	K 7 22		Roth. 61	
Circle, The 2	O11 36		Club St. 11	K12 34		Conduit La. 10	J10 34
City Rd. 2	M11 35		Clumber Rd. 10	G11 33		Conduit Rd. 10	J10 34
Clara St., Roth. 61	R 5 16		Clun Rd. 4	M 9 23		Congress St. 1	K10 34
Clarefield Rd. 9	O 8 24		Clun St. 4	M 9 23		Portobello St.	
Claremont Cres. 10	J10 34		Clyde Rd. 8	K13 44		Coningsby Rd. 5	M 7 23
Claremont Pl. 10	J10 34		Coach Rd., Roth. 61	R 2 6		Coniston Rd. 8	K13 44
Claremont St., Roth. 65	Q 5 15		Coal Pit La. 6	G 7 21		Coniston Ter. 8	K13 44
Clarence La. 3	K11 34		Coal Pit Pla., Wor. 30	E 5 10		Coniston Rd.	
Clarence Rd. 6	H 8 21		Coal Riding La.,	W 5 18		Constable Clo. 14	N15 46
Clarendon Dr. 10	G12 33		Dal.M. 65			Constable Clo.,	X 5 19
Clarendon Rd. 10	G12 33		Coalbrook Av. 13	S12 38		Bram. 66	
Clarendon Rd., Roth. 65	T 4 17		Coalbrook Gro. 13	S12 38		Constable Dr. 14	M15 45
Clark Gro., Stan. 6	F 9 20		Coalbrook Rd. 13	S12 38		Constable Pl. 14	N15 46

86

Name	Ref	Pg
Constable Rd. 14	M15	45
Constable Way 14	M15	45
Constantine Av. 60	S 7	26
Brin. 60		
Convent Wk. 3	K10	34
Cavendish St.		
Conway Cres., Roth. 65	V 4	18
Conway St. 3	K10	34
Cooks Rd. 19	U15	49
Cooks Wood Rd. 3	L 8	23
Cookson Clo. 5	J 6	12
Cookson Rd. 5	J 6	12
Coombe Pl. 10	J10	34
Coombe Rd. 10	H10	33
Copper St. 3	L10	35
Coppice Gdns., Roth. 61	R 3	6
Coppice La., Stan. 6	E10	32
Coppice Rd. 10	E10	32
Coppice Vw. 10	G10	33
Coppice, The, Roth. 61	P 3	5
Coppin Sq. 5	K 4	12
Corby Rd. 4	N 7	24
Corby St. 4	M 9	23
Corker Bottoms La. 2	N10	36
Corker Rd. 12	O13	46
Cornish St. 6	K 9	22
Coronation Bridge,	R 5	16
Roth. 60		
Coronation Rd., Raw. 62	V 1	8
Corporation St. 3	L10	35
Corporation St.,	S 5	16
Roth. 60		
Cortworth Rd. 11	H14	43
Corwen Pl. 13	R13	48
Cossey Rd. 4	M 9	23
Cotleigh Av. 12	R14	48
Cotleigh Clo. 12	R14	48
Cotleigh Cres. 12	R14	48
Cotleigh Dr. 12	R14	48
Cotleigh Gdns. 12	R14	48
Cotleigh Pl. 12	R14	48
Cotleigh Rd. 12	R14	48
Cotleigh Way 12	R14	48
Cotswold Cres.,	V 7	28
Whis. 60		
Cotswold Rd. 6	H 8	21
Cottage La. 11	F13	42
Cottam Clo., Whis. 60	V 7	28
Cottenham Rd., Roth. 60	T 4	17
Cottingham St. 9	N 9	24
Cotton Mill Row 3	L 9	23
Cotton Mill Wk. 3	L 9	23
Alma St.		
Cotton St. 3	L 9	23
Coulston St. 3	L10	35
West Bar		
Countess Rd. 1	L11	35
St. Marys Rd.		
Countess St. 1	L11	35
Coupe Rd. 3	L 9	23
Coupland Rd., Roth. 65	V 4	18
Coventry Rd. 9	P 9	25
Coverdale Rd. 7	K13	44
Cow La. 11	H12	33
Cow La. 11	H14	43
Coward Dr. 30	F 4	10
Cowdrey Cres., Roth. 61	Q 4	15
Cowley Gdns., Mosb. 19	T16	59
Cowley Rd., Ought. 30	F 5	10
Cowlishaw Rd. 11	J12	34
Cowper Av. 6	J 5	12
Cowper Cres. 3	J 5	12
Cowper Dr. 6	J 5	12
Cowper Dr., Roth. 65	V 4	18
Cowrakes Clo., Whis. 60	V 7	28
Cowrakes La., Whis. 60	V 7	28
Cowslip Rd. 5	N 6	14
Cox Pl. 6	G 7	21
Cox Rd. 6	G 7	21
Crabtree Av. 5	M 7	23
Crabtree Clo.		
Crabtree Clo. 5	M 7	23
Crabtree Cres. 5	L 7	23
Crabtree Dr. 5	M 7	23
Crabtree La. 5	L 7	23
Crabtree Pl. 5	L 7	23
Crabtree Rd. 5	L 8	23
Cradock Rd. 2	N12	36
Crag View Clo.,	F 4	10
Ought. 30		
Crag View Cres.,	F 4	10
Ought. 30		
Cragdale Gro. 19	S16	58
Crane Dr., Roth. 61	Q 4	15
Crane Rd., Roth. 61	Q 3	5
Cranford Clo. 19	R14	48
Cranford Dr.		
Cranford Ct., Hack. 19	R15	48
Cranford Dr., Hack. 19	R14	48
Cranworth Pl. 3	L 9	23
Cranworth Rd. 3	L 9	23
Cranworth Rd., Roth. 65	T 4	17
Craven Clo. 9	P 9	25
York Rd.		
Craven St. 3	K10	34
Craven St., Raw. 62	T 2	7
Crawford Rd. 8	K14	44
Crawshaw Av. 8	J16	54
Crawshaw Gro. 8	J16	54
Cream St. 2	L11	35
Creighton Av., Raw. 62	U 1	7
Crescent East, The,	Y 5	19
Bram. 66		
Crescent Rd. 7	K12	34
Crescent West, The,	X 4	19
Bram. 66		
Crescent, The, Roth. 65	T 4	17
Crescent, The, Tot. 17	G17	53
Cresswell Rd. 9	P10	37
Crest Rd. 5	L 6	13
Crestwood Ct. 5	M 6	13
Crestwood Gdns. 5	M 6	13
Creswick Av. 30	K 4	12
Creswick Clo., Roth. 65	V 4	18
Creswick Greave Clo. 5	K 4	12
Creswick La., Gren. 30	K 4	12
Creswick Rd., Roth. 65	V 4	18
Creswick St. 6	J 9	22
Creswick Way 6	J 9	22
Creswick St.		
Cricket Inn Cres. 2	N10	36
Cricket Inn Rd. 2	M10	35
Crimicar Av. 10	E12	32
Crimicar Clo. 10	F12	32
Crimicar Dr. 10	E12	32
Crimicar La. 10	E11	32
Crispin Clo. 12	O14	46
Crispin Dr. 12	O14	46
Crispin Gdns. 12	O14	46
Crispin Rd. 12	O14	46
Croft Clo. 11	G14	43
Croft La. 11	G14	43
Croft Lea, D.Wd. 18	J18	54
Croft Rd. 12	O13	46
Croft Rd., Brin. 60	R 7	26
Croft Rd., Stan. 6	F 9	20
Croft St., Roth. 61	R 2	6
Croft, The, Wick. 66	X 6	19
Crofton Av. 6	H 7	21
Crofts Dr., Thry. 65	W 3	8
Crofts, The, Roth. 60	S 5	16
Cromford St. 2	L11	35
Cromwell St. 6	J 9	22
Crooked La., Hoot.R. 65	Y 1	9
Crookes 10	H10	33
Crookes Rd. 10	J10	34
Crookes Valley Rd. 10	J10	34
Crookesmoor Rd. 6 & 10	J10	34
Crosby Rd. 8	K14	44
Cross Allen Rd. 18	T15	49
Cross Bedford St. 6	K 9	22
Cross Burgess St.	L10	35
Cambridge St.		
Cross Chantry Rd. 8	L14	45
Cross Dr. 13	R13	48
Cross Gilpin St. 6	K 9	22
Gilpin St.		
Cross Hill, Eccl. 30	M 4	13
Cross House Rd.,	J 4	12
Gren. 30		
Cross La. 10	H10	33
Cross La., C.A. 18	M17	55
Cross La., C.A. 18	M18	55
Cross La., Dore 17	F16	52
Cross Love St. 3	L10	35
Love St.		
Cross Myrtle Rd. 2	L12	35
Cross Park Rd. 8	L13	45
Cross Smithfield 3	K10	34
Cross St. Roth. 61	R 5	16
Cross St., Bram. 66	Y 5	19
Cross St., Greas. 61	S 2	6
Cross St., Raw. 62	T 2	7
Cross St., Thur. 66	Y 8	29
Cross St., Wood. 13	R13	48
Cross Turner St. 2	L11	35
Cross Wk. 11	K11	34
London Rd.		
Crossland Dr. 12	O14	46
Crossland Pl. 12	O14	46
Crossways, The 2	O11	36
Crowder Av. 5	K 6	12
Crowder Clo. 5	L 6	13
Crowder Cres. 5	L 6	13
Crowder Rd. 5	L 6	13
Crowland Rd. 5	L 6	13
Crown Clo., Roth. 61	Q 4	15
Crown Hill Rd.,	R 7	26
Brin. 60		
Crown Pl. 2	M10	35
Duke St.		
Crowther Pl. 7	L12	35
Croydon St. 11	K12	34
Langdon St.		
Cruise Rd. 11	G12	33
Crummock Rd. 8	K13	44
Crumpsall Dr. 5	K 7	22
Crumpsall Rd. 5	K 7	22
Crumwell Rd.,	P 3	5
Roth. 61		
Cullabine Rd. 2	O12	36
Cumberland St. 1	L11	35
Cumberland Way 1	L11	35
Cundy St. 6	J 9	22
Cunliffe St., C.A. 18	M18	55
Cupola 3	L10	35
Gibraltar St.		
Curlew Dr., Th.Hes. 61	O 1	4
Curlew Ridge 2	N11	36
Skye Edge Av.		
Cuthbert Bank 6	J 8	22
Cuthbert Bank Rd. 6	J 8	22
Cuthbert Rd. 6	J 8	22
Langsett St.		
Cutts Ter. 8	K12	34
Cyclops St. 4	N 8	24
Cypress Av. 8	M15	45
Cyprus Rd. 8	L13	45
Cyprus Ter. 6	J 9	22
Burgoyne Rd.		
Dacre Row 2	M10	35
St. Johns Rd.		
Daffodil Rd. 5	N 6	14
Dagnam Clo. 2	N13	46
Dagnam Cres. 2	N13	46
Dagnam Dr. 2	N12	36
Dagnam Pl. 2	N13	46
Dagnam Rd. 2	N12	36
Daisy Bank 3	K10	34
Daisy St., Roth. 60	S 4	16
Daisy Wk. 19	T14	49
Daisy Wk. 3	K10	34
Dale Av., Roth. 65	V 5	18
Dale Rd., Raw. 62	T 1	7
Dale Rd., Roth. 65	V 6	18
Dale Rd., Wick. 66	X 5	19
Dale St., Raw. 62	T 1	7
Dale, The 8	K14	44
Daleview Rd. 8	J15	44
Dalewood Av. 8	J15	44
Dalewood Dr. 8	J15	44
Dalewood Rd. 8	J15	44

88

Street	Grid	Map
Dunlop St. 9	O 7	24
Dunmow Rd. 4	N 7	24
Dunning Rd. 5	M 4	13
Dunning Ter. 5	M 4	13
Durham La. 10	K10	34
Durham Rd.		
Durham Pl., Roth. 65	U 6	17
Durham Rd. 10	J10	34
Durlstone Clo. 12	O13	46
Durlstone Cres. 12	O13	46
Durlstone Dr. 12	O13	46
Durlstone Gro. 12	O13	46
Durmast Gro., Stan. 6	F 9	20
Durvale Ct. 17	G17	53
Dutton Rd. 6	J 7	22
Dyche Clo. 8	L17	55
Dyche Dr. 8	L17	55
Dyche La. 8	L16	55
Dyche La., C.A. 18	L17	55
Dyche Pl. 8	L17	55
Dyche Rd. 8	L17	55
Dycott Rd., Roth. 61	Q 4	15
Dyke Vale Av. 12	R14	48
Dyke Vale Clo. 12	R14	48
Dyke Vale Pl. 12	R14	48
Dyke Vale Rd. 12	R14	48
Dyke Vale Way 12	R14	48
Dykes Hall Gdns. 6	H 8	21
Dykes Hall Pl. 6	H 7	21
Dykes Hall Rd. 6	H 7	21
Dykes La. 6	H 8	21
Dykewood Dr. 6	G 6	11
Dyson Pl. 11	J12	34
Sharrow Vale Rd.		
Earl Marshal Clo. 4	M 7	23
Earl Marshal Dr. 4	M 7	23
Earl Marshal Rd. 4	N 7	24
Earl Marshal Vw. 4	M 8	23
Earl St. 1	L11	35
Earl Way 1	L11	35
Earldom Clo. 4	M 9	23
Earldom Dr. 4	M 9	23
Earldom Rd. 4	M 8	23
Earldom St. 4	M 9	23
Earsham St. 4	M 9	23
East Av., Raw. 62	T 1	7
East Bank Clo. 2	M13	45
East Bank Pl. 2	M13	45
East Bank Rd. 2	L11	35
East Bank Vw. 2	M13	45
East Bank Way 2	M13	45
East Bawtry Rd., Roth. 60	U 7	27
East Coast Rd. 9	N 9	24
East Cres., Roth. 65	U 4	17
East Glade Av. 12	Q14	47
East Glade Clo. 12	Q14	47
East Glade Cres. 12	Q14	47
East Glade Pl. 12	Q14	47
East Glade Rd. 12	Q14	47
East Glade Sq. 12	Q14	47
East Glade Way 12	Q14	47
East Par. 1	L10	35
High St.		
East Rd. 2	L12	35
East Rd., Roth. 65	U 4	17
East View Dr., Thry. 65	W 3	8
Eastcroft Clo., Mosb. 19	T16	59
Eastcroft Dr., Mosb. 19	T16	59
Eastcroft Glen, Mosb. 19	T16	59
Eastcroft Vw., Mosb. 19	T16	59
Eastcroft Way, Mosb. 19	T16	59
Eastern Av. 2	N12	36
Eastern Cres. 2	M13	45
Eastern Dr. 2	M12	35
Eastern Wk. 2	M12	35
Eastfield Pl., Raw. 62	V 1	8
Eastgrove Rd. 10	J11	34
Eastview Ter. 6	H 7	21
Leader Rd.		
Eastwood La., Roth. 65	T 4	17
Eastwood Mt., Roth. 65	U 5	17
Eastwood Rd. 11	J12	34
Eaton Pl. 2	M10	35
Eben St. 9	O 7	24
Ebenezer Pl. 3	L 9	23
Green La.		
Ebenezer St. 3	L 9	23
Eccles St. 9	O 6	14
Ecclesall Rd. 11	H12	33
Ecclesall Rd. S. 11	G15	43
Ecclesfield Rd. 5 & 9	M 4	13
Eckington Rd. 19	U15	49
Eckington Rd., C.A. 18	M18	55
Eckington Way 19	T16	59
Edale Rd. 11	H13	43
Edale Rd., Roth. 61	Q 5	15
Eden Cres. 6	G 8	21
Eden Dr. 6	G 8	21
Edenhall Rd. 2	N12	36
Edensor Rd. 5	L 7	23
Edge Bank 7	K13	44
Machon Bank Rd.		
Edge Clo. 6	J 5	12
Edge La. 6	J 5	12
Edge Well Clo. 6	J 5	12
Edge Well Cres. 6	J 5	12
Edge Well Dr. 6	J 5	12
Edge Well Pl. 6	J 5	12
Edge Well Ri. 6	J 5	12
Edge Well Way 6	J 5	12
Edgebrook Rd. 7	J13	44
Edgedale Rd. 7	K13	44
Edgefield Rd. 7	K13	44
Edgehill Rd. 7	J13	44
Edgemount Rd. 7	K13	44
Edmund Av. 17	J17	54
Edmund Av., Brin. 60	S 8	26
Edmund Clo. 17	J17	54
Edmund Dr. 17	J17	54
Edmund Rd. 2	L12	35
Edward St. 3	K10	34
Edwin Rd. 2	M13	45
Effingham La. 4	M10	35
Effingham Rd. 4 & 9	M 9	23
Effingham Sq., Roth. 65	S 4	16
Effingham St. 4	M 9	23
Effingham St., Roth. 65	S 5	16
Egerton La. 1	K11	34
Egerton St. 1	K11	34
Eilam Clo., Roth. 61	Q 4	15
Eilam Rd., Roth. 61	Q 4	15
Elcroft Gdns., Btn. 19	T15	58
Elder Dr., Bram. 66	X 5	19
Eldertree Rd., Th.Hes. 61	N 2	4
Eldon Ct. 1	K10	34
Eldon Rd., Roth. 65	T 4	17
Eldon St. 1	K10	34
Eleanor St. 9	O 9	24
Elgin St. 10	H10	33
Ella Rd. 4	M 8	23
Ellen St., Roth. 61	R 4	16
Ellenborough Rd. 6	H 8	21
Ellerton Rd. 5	M 7	23
Ellesmere Rd. 4	M 9	23
Ellesmere Rd. N. 4	M 8	23
Ellesmere Wk. 4	M 8	23
Ellin St. 1	L11	35
Elliot Dr., Roth. 61	Q 3	5
Elliott Rd. 6	J10	34
Elliottville St. 6	J 9	22
Walkley Bank Rd.		
Ellis St. 3	K10	34
Ellis St., Brin. 60	S 7	26
Ellison St. 3	K10	34
Elm Cres. 19	S16	58
Elm La. 5	L 6	13
Elm Pl., Raw. 62	U 1	7
Elm Rd. 19	U14	49
Elm View Rd. 9	O 6	14
Elmfield Av. 5	L 6	13
Elmham Rd. 9	P10	37
Elmhirst Dr., Roth. 65	V 6	18
Elmore Rd. 10	J10	34
Elmtree Cres. 18	L18	55
Elmtree Rd., Th.Hes. 61	N 2	4
Elmwood Dr. 19	S17	58
Elsham Clo., Rav. 65	Y 4	19
Elstree Dr. 12	O14	46
Elstree Rd. 12	O14	46
Elwood Rd. 17	J17	54
Embankment Rd. 10	J10	34
Emerson Clo. 5	L 5	13
Emerson Cres. 5	L 6	13
Emerson Dr. 5	L 6	13
Emily Rd. 7	K13	44
Empire Rd. 7	K12	34
Endcliffe Av. 10	J11	34
Endcliffe Cres. 10	H11	33
Endcliffe Edge 10	H11	33
Endcliffe Vale Rd.		
Endcliffe Glen Rd. 11	J11	34
Endcliffe Grove Av. 10	H11	33
Endcliffe Hall Av. 10	H11	33
Endcliffe Rise Rd. 11	J11	34
Endcliffe Terrace Rd. 11	J11	34
Endcliffe Vale Av. 11	J12	34
Endcliffe Vale Rd. 10	H11	33
Endfield Rd. 5	K 4	12
Endowood Rd. 7	H15	43
Enfield Pl. 13	Q11	37
Ennerdale Av. 19	T17	59
Ennerdale Dr. 19	T17	59
Epping Gdns., Btn. 19	U15	49
Epping Gro., Btn. 19	U15	49
Errington Av. 2	N12	36
Errington Clo. 2	N13	46
Errington Cres. 2	N13	46
Errington Rd. 2	N13	46
Errington Way 2	N12	36
Erskine Cres. 2	M12	35
Erskine Rd. 2	M12	35
Erskine Rd., Roth. 65	T 4	17
Erskine Vw. 2	M12	35
Eskdale Clo. 6	J 6	12
Eskdale Rd. 6	J 6	12
Eskdale Rd., Roth. 61	Q 2	5
Esperanto Pl. 1	L10	35
Flat St.		
Essendine Cres. 8	L14	45
Essex Rd. 2	M11	35
Etwall Way 5	M 6	13
Evans St. 3	K11	34
Evelyn Rd. 10	H10	33
Everard Av. 17	H17	53
Everard Clo. 17	H17	53
Everard Dr. 17	H17	53
Everard Glade 17	H17	53
Everingham Clo. 5	L 6	13
Everingham Cres. 5	K 6	12
Everingham Rd. 5	L 6	13
Everton Rd. 11	J12	34
Evesham Clo. 9	O 6	14
Ewers Rd., Roth. 61	Q 5	15
Exchange Gateway 1	L10	35
Fargate		
Exchange Pl. 2	L10	34
Exchange St.		
Exchange St. 2	L10	35
Exeter Dr. 3	K11	34
Exeter Pl. 3	K11	34
Exeter Way 3	K11	34
Exley Av. 6	J 9	22
Eyam Rd. 10	H10	33
Eyncourt Rd. 5	M 6	13
Eyre La. 1	L11	35
Eyre St. 1	L11	35
Fabian Way, Bram. 66	Y 6	19
Fairbank Rd. 5	L 7	23
Fairbank Vw., Whis. 60	V 7	28
Fairbarn Dr. 6	G 9	21
Fairbarn Clo. 6	G 9	21
Fairbarn Pl. 6	G 9	21
Fairbarn Rd. 6	G 9	21
Fairbarn Way 6	G 9	21
Fairfax Rd. 2	O12	36
Fairleigh 2	O12	36
Fairleigh Dr., Roth. 60	T 6	17
Fairmount Gdns. 12	R14	48

89

Place	Ref	Page
France St. 62	T2	7
Francis Cres. N., Roth. 60	V6	18
Francis Cres. S., Roth. 60	V6	18
Francis Dr., Roth. 60	V6	18
Francis St., Roth. 60	T5	17
Frank Pl. 9	O8	24
Stovin Clo.		
Fraser Clo. 8	K14	44
Fraser Cres. 8	K14	44
Fraser Dr. 8	K14	44
Fraser Rd. 8	K14	44
Fraser Rd., Roth. 60	T5	17
Fraser Wk. 8	K14	44
Fraser Cres.		
Frederick Rd. 7	K12	34
Frederick St. 9	O9	24
Frederick St., Roth. 60 & 65	S4	16
Frederick St., Cat. 60	S9	26
Freeborough St. 9	O9	24
Freedom Ct. 6	J8	22
Freedom Rd. 6	J9	22
Freedom St. 6	J8	22
Burnaby St.		
Freeman Rd., Wick. 66	X5	19
Freeston Pl. 9	O8	24
Leigh La.		
Fretson Rd. 2	O12	36
Fretwell Rd., Roth. 65	V4	18
Friar Clo., Stan. 6	F9	20
Frickley Rd. 11	G12	33
Frith Clo. 12	O13	46
Frith Rd. 12	O13	46
Frog Wk. 11	K12	34
Froggatt La. 1	L11	35
Frogmore Clo., Bram. 66	Y5	19
Front St., Tree. 60	T10	39
Fulford Clo. 9	P9	25
Fulford Pl. 9	P9	25
Fullerton Cres., Thry. 65	W3	8
Fullerton Dr., Brin. 60	R8	26
Fullerton Rd., Roth. 60	S6	16
Fulmar Way, Th.Hes. 61	O1	4
Fulmer Rd. 11	J12	34
Fulmere Cres. 5	K5	12
Fulmere Rd. 5	K5	12
Fulney Rd. 11	G12	33
Fulton Rd. 6	J9	22
Fulwood Head Rd. 10	C12	31
Fulwood La. 11	C13	41
Fulwood Rd. 10	F12	32
Furnace Hill 3	L10	35
Furnace La. 13	T12	39
Furness Clo., Stan. 6	F8	20
Furniss Av. 17	F17	52
Furnival Gate 1	L11	35
Furnival Rd. 4	L10	35
Furnival St. 1	L11	35
Furnival Way, Whis. 60	V7	28
Gainsborough Clo., Bram. 66	X5	19
Gainsborough Rd. 11	J12	34
Gainsford Rd. 9	P10	37
Galley Dr. 19	S15	48
Gallow Tree Rd., Roth. 65	V6	18
Galsworthy Av. 5	K6	12
Galsworthy Rd. 5	K7	22
Galway Clo., Raw. 62	U1	7
Gamston Rd. 8	K12	34
Ganton Rd. 6	H7	21
Garbroards Cres., Thry. 65	W3	8
Garden Cres., Roth. 60	U7	27
Garden La., Rav. 65	Y2	9
Garden St. 1	K10	34
Garden St., Roth. 61	R4	16
Garden Wk., Btn. 19	U14	49
Garfield Mt. 65	T5	17
Alfred St.		
Garland Cft., Mosb. 19	T16	59
Garland Clo., Mosb. 19	T16	59
Garland Dr., Lox. 6	F7	20
Garland Mt., Mosb. 19	T16	59
Garland Way, Mosb. 19	T16	59
Garry Rd. 6	H7	21
Garter St. 4	M8	23
Garth Rd. 9	O9	24
Gashouse La., Eck. 31	S17	58
Gate Wk. 9	P10	37
Main Rd.		
Gatefield Rd. 7	K13	44
Gateway, The 62	S3	6
Mangham Rd.		
Gatty Rd. 5	M4	13
Gaunt Clo. 14	M14	45
Gaunt Dr. 14	M14	45
Gaunt Pl. 14	M14	45
Gaunt Rd. 14	M14	45
Gaunt Way 14	M14	45
Gayton Rd. 4	M8	23
Geer La., Ridg. 12	P17	57
Gell St. 3	K10	34
George St. 1	L10	35
George St., Roth. 60	S4	16
Georges Pl., Raw. 62	U1	7
Gerard Clo. 8	L13	45
Carrfield St.		
Gerard Rd., Roth. 60	T5	17
Gerard St. 8	L13	45
Gerrard Av., Thry. 65	X3	9
Gertrude St. 6	K9	22
Gervase Av. 8	K17	54
Gervase Dr. 8	K17	54
Gervase Pl. 8	K17	54
Gervase Rd. 8	K17	54
Gervase Wk. 8	K17	54
Gibbing Greaves Rd., Roth. 65	W6	18
Gibbons Dr. 14	N15	46
Gibbons Wk. 14	N15	46
Gibraltar St. 3	L10	35
Gifford Rd. 8	L12	35
Gilberthorpe Dr., Roth. 65	U5	17
Gilberthorpe St., Roth. 65	T5	17
Gill Clo., Wick. 66	X6	19
Gill Croft 6	F9	20
Gill Meadows		
Gill Meadows 6	F9	20
Gilleyfield Av. 17	G16	53
Gillott Hill 6	J6	12
Fox Hill Rd.		
Gillott La., Wick. 66	X6	19
Gillott Rd. 6	J6	12
Gilpin La. 6	K9	22
Infirmary Rd.		
Gilpin St. 6	K9	22
Ginhouse La., Roth. 61	S4	16
Girton Rd. 9	O8	24
Gisborne Rd. 11	H13	43
Glade, The 10	H11	33
Gladstone Rd. 10	G11	33
Gladys St., Roth. 65	U5	17
Glasshouse La., Kiln. 62	W1	8
Glasshouse St., Roth. 60	S4	16
Glave St. 9	O8	24
Gleadless Av. 12	O14	46
Gleadless Bank 12	N14	46
Gleadless Common 12	N13	46
Gleadless Cres. 12	N13	46
Gleadless Dr. 12	N14	46
Gleadless Mt. 12	O14	46
Gleadless Rd. 2 & 12	L12	35
Glebe Cres., Thry. 65	W3	8
Glebe Rd. 10	J10	34
Glen Rd. 7	K13	44
Glen View Rd. 8	K16	54
Glen Wy. 11	G12	33
Hanging Water Rd.		
Glen, The 11	H11	33
Glenalmond Rd. 11	H12	33
Glencoe Dr. 2	M11	35
Glencoe Pl. 2	M11	35
Glencoe Rd. 2	M11	35
Glenholme Dr. 13	Q12	37
Glenholme Pl. 13	Q12	37
Glenholme Rd. 13	Q12	37
Glenholme Way 13	Q12	37
Glenmore Cft. 12	P13	47
Glenorchy Rd. 7	J13	44
Glentilt Rd. 7	J13	44
Glossop La. 10	K10	34
Glossop Rd. 10	J11	34
Glossop Row, Ought. 30	F4	10
Church St.		
Gloucester Cres. 10	K11	34
Gloucester St.		
Gloucester Rd. 61	Q3	5
Gloucester St. 10	K11	34
Glover Rd. 8	L12	35
Glover Rd., Tot. 17	G18	53
Goathland Clo. 13	S12	38
Goathland Dr. 13	S12	38
Goathland Pl. 13	S12	38
Goathland Rd. 13	S12	38
Goddard Hall Rd. 5	M7	23
Godric Rd. 5	M4	13
Godric Rd., Brin. 60	R7	26
Godstone Rd., Roth. 60	T5	17
Goldcrest Wk., Th.Hes. 61	O1	4
Golden Oak Dell 6	E8	20
Acorn Dr.		
Goldsmith Dr., Roth. 65	U5	17
Goldsmith Rd., Roth. 65	U5	17
Goodison Cres. 6	G9	21
Goodison Ri. 6	G9	21
Goodwin Av., Raw. 62	T1	7
Goodwin Rd. 8	L13	45
Thirlwell Rd.		
Goodwin Rd., Roth. 61	R2	6
Goore Av. 9	O11	36
Goore Dr. 9	O10	36
Goore Rd. 9	O11	36
Goose La., Wick. 66	Y6	19
Goosebutt St. 62	T2	7
Goosecroft Av., Thry. 65	W3	8
Gordon Av. 8	L14	45
Mount View Rd.		
Gordon Rd. 11	J12	34
Gorse La. 10	D12	31
Gorse, The, Wick. 66	X6	19
Gorseland Ct., Wick. 66	X6	19
Gosber St., Eck. 31	S18	58
Gotham Rd., Brin. 60	S7	26
Gough Clo., Roth. 65	V6	18
Gough St., Roth. 60	S4	16
Goulder Pl. 9	O8	24
Attercliffe Common		
Goulder Ter. 9	O7	24
Attercliffe Common		
Gower St. 4	M9	23
Grafton St. 2	M11	35
Graham Av., Brin. 60	S8	26
Howarth Rd.		
Graham Rd. 10	G11	33
Grammar St. 6	J9	22
Granby Rd. 5	M7	23
Grange Cliffe Clo. 11	H14	43
Grange Cres. 11	K12	34
Grange Crescent Rd. 11	K12	34
Grange Dr., Roth. 61	P3	5
Grange Farm Dr. 6	F6	10
Grange La. 13	R12	38
Grange La., Roth. 60	R6	16
Grange La., Roth. 61	N4	14
Grange Mill La., Roth. 61	N4	14
Grange Rd. 11	K12	34
Grange Rd., Btn. 19	T14	49
Grange Rd., Raw. 62	U1	7
Grange Rd., Roth. 60	U6	17
Grange View Cres., Roth. 61	P4	15

Name	Grid	Pg
Hammerton Clo. 6	J 8	22
Hammerton Rd. 6	J 8	22
Hammond St. 3	K10	34
Hampton Rd. 5	M 7	23
Handley St. 3	L 9	23
Hands Rd. 10	J10	34
Handsworth Av. 9	P10	37
Handsworth Cres. 9	P10	37
Handsworth Grange Clo. 13	R11	38
Handsworth Grange Cres. 13	R11	38
Handsworth Grange Dr. 13	R11	38
Handsworth Grange Rd. 13	R11	38
Handsworth Grange Way 13	R11	38
Handsworth Rd. 9 & 13	Q10	37
Hangingwater Clo. 10	G12	33
Hangingwater Rd. 11	G12	33
Hangram La. 11	E14	42
Hanmoor Rd., Stan. 6	F 9	20
Hannah Rd. 13	S12	38
Hanover Ct. 3	K11	34
Hanover Sq. 3	K11	34
Hanover St. 3	K11	34
Hanover Way 3	K11	34
Hanson Rd., Lox. 6	F 8	20
Harbord Rd. 8	K15	44
Harborough Av. 2	O11	36
Harborough Clo. 2	O11	36
Harborough Dr. 2	O11	36
Harborough Rd. 2	O11	36
Harborough Ri. 2	O11	36
Harborough Way 2	O11	36
Harbury St. 13	T12	39
Harcourt Cres. 10	J10	34
Harcourt Rd.		
Harcourt Rd. 10	J10	34
Hardcastle Dr. 13	R12	38
Hardcastle Gdns. 13	R12	38
Hardcastle Rd. 13	R13	48
Hardie Pl., Raw. 62	T 1	7
Harding St. 9	O 9	24
Hardwick Clo., Dron. 18	L18	55
Hardwick Cres. 11	J12	34
Hardwick St., Roth. 65	V 4	18
Hardwicke Rd., Roth. 65	T 4	17
Hardy Pl. 6	J 9	22
Hardy St., Roth. 60	S 4	16
Harefield Rd. 11	J11	34
Harehills Rd., Roth. 60	T 5	17
Harewood Gro., Bram. 66	Y 5	19
Harewood Rd. 8	J 7	22
Harewood Way 11	H15	43
Harland Rd. 11	K11	34
Harleston St. 4	M 9	23
Harley Rd. 11	G13	43
Harmer La. 1	L10	35
Harney Clo. 9	P 9	25
Harold Croft, Roth. 61	S 2	6
Harold St. 6	J 9	22
Harpur House, Roth. 65	T 4	17
Harrington Pl. 2	L12	35
Harrington Rd. 2	L12	35
Harris Rd. 6	H 7	21
Harrison La. 10	E12	32
Harrison Rd. 6	H 8	21
Harrop La. 10	D13	41
Harrow St. 11	K11	34
Harrowden Ct. 9	Q 7	25
Harrowden Rd. 9	Q 7	25
Harry Firth Clo. 9	O 9	24
Hartford Clo. 8	L14	45
Hartford Rd. 8	L14	45
Harthill Rd. 13	O12	36
Hartington Av. 7	J14	44
Hartington Clo., Roth. 61	R 5	16
Hartington Rd. 7	J14	44
Hartington Rd., Dron. 18	L18	55

Name	Grid	Pg
Hartington Rd., Roth. 61	R 5	16
Hartland Av. 19	U15	49
Hartland Ct. 19	U15	49
Hartland Dr. 19	U15	49
Hartley Brook 5	M 4	13
Hartley Brook Av. 5	M 5	13
Hartley Brook Rd. 5	M 5	13
Hartley La., Roth. 61	S 4	16
Hartley St. 2	L12	35
Hartopp Av. 2	M13	45
Hartopp Clo. 2	M13	45
Hartopp Dr. 2	M13	45
Hartopp Rd. 2	M13	45
Hartshead 1	L10	35
Harvest La. 3	L 9	23
Harvest Rd., Wick. 66	X 5	19
Harvey Clough Rd. 8	L14	45
Harwell Rd. 8	K12	34
Harwich Rd. 2	N11	36
Harwood Clo. 2	L12	35
Harwood Dr. 19	T15	49
Harwood Gdns. 19	T15	49
Harwood St. 2	L12	35
Haslam Cres. 8	J17	54
Haslehurst Rd. 2	N11	36
Hastilar Clo. 2	O12	36
Hastilar Dr. 2	P12	37
Hastilar Rd. 2	O12	36
Hastilar Rd. S. 13	P12	37
Hastings Mt. 7	J14	44
Hastings Rd. 7	J14	44
Hatfield House Cft. 5	M 5	13
Hatfield House Ct. 5	M 5	13
Hatfield House La. 5	M 6	13
Hatherley Rd. 9	Q 6	15
Hatherley Rd., Roth. 65	T 4	17
Hathersage Rd. 17	E15	42
Hatton Rd. 6	J 8	22
Langsett Rd.		
Haugh La. 11	G14	43
Haugh Rd., Raw. 62	S 1	6
Haughton Rd. 8	K15	44
Havelock St. 10	K11	34
Havercroft Rd. 8	K14	44
Havercroft Rd., Roth. 60	V 6	18
Hawke St. 9	O 8	24
Hawkshead Rd. 4	N 7	24
Hawksley Av. 6	J 8	22
Hawksley Rd. 6	J 8	22
Hawksley Ri., Ought. 30	F 5	10
Hawksworth Clo., Roth. 65	V 4	18
Hawksworth Rd. 6	J 9	22
Hawksworth Rd., Roth. 65	V 4	18
Hawley St. 1	L10	35
Hawley St., Raw. 62	T 1	7
Haworth Bank, Roth. 60	T 7	27
Haworth Cres., Roth. 60	T 7	27
Haworth La., Whis. 60	T 8	27
Hawthorn Av. 19	S15	48
Hawthorn Av., Raw. 62	U 1	7
Hawthorn Rd. 6	H 8	21
Hawthorn St. 6	H 8	21
Hawthorn Ter. 10	J10	34
Parkers La.		
Hawthorne Av., Dron. 18	L18	55
Haxby Clo. 13	Q13	47
Haxby Pl. 13	Q13	47
Haxby St. 13	Q13	47
Haybrook Ct. 17	G17	53
Haydon Gro., Bram. 66	X 5	19
Hayes St. 19	T17	59
Hayes Dr. 19	T17	59
Hayfield Cres. 12	P14	47
Hayfield Dr. 12	P14	47
Hayfield Pl. 12	P14	47
Hayland St. 9	O 7	24
Haymarket 1	L10	35
Haywood Clo., Roth. 65	V 4	18
Hazel Gro., Bram. 66	Y 5	19

Name	Grid	Pg
Hazelbadge Cres. 12	Q14	47
Hazelbarrow Clo. 8	M16	55
Hazelbarrow Cres. 8	L16	55
Hazelbarrow Dr. 8	L16	55
Hazelbarrow Gro. 8	M16	55
Hazelbarrow Rd. 8	L17	55
Hazelhurst La. 8	N16	56
Headford St. 3	K11	34
Headland Dr. 10	H10	33
Headland Rd. 10	H10	33
Heath Rd. 6	J 6	12
Heathcote St. 4	M 7	23
Owler La.		
Heather Lea Av. 17	F16	52
Heather Lea Pl. 17	F16	52
Heather Rd. 5	N 6	14
Heathfield Rd. 12	P14	47
Heatons Bank, Raw. 62	U 1	7
Heavygate Av. 10	H 9	21
Heavygate Rd. 10	J 9	22
Heeley Bank 2	L12	35
Myrtle Rd.		
Heeley Bank Rd. 2	L12	35
Heeley Grn. 2	L13	45
Hellaby Vw., Rav. 65	Y 4	19
Helmsley Av. 19	T16	59
Helmton Dr. 8	L14	45
Helmton Rd. 8	K15	44
Helston Ri. 7	J14	44
Hemper Gro. 8	J17	54
Hemper La. 8	J17	54
Hemsworth Rd. 8	L15	45
Hendon St. 13	Q11	37
Henley Av. 8	L16	55
Henley Grove Rd., Roth. 61	R 4	16
Henley La., Roth. 61	R 4	16
Henley St., Roth. 61	R 4	16
Henley Way, Roth. 61	R 4	16
Henry St. 3	K 9	22
Henry St., Eck. 31	S18	58
Henry St., Raw. 62	T 2	7
Henry St., Roth. 65	S 4	16
Henson St. 9	O 9	24
Heppenstall La. 9	N 9	24
Herbert Rd. 7	K13	44
Herbert St., Roth. 61	Q 4	15
Herdings Ct. 12	O14	46
Herdings Rd. 12	O14	46
Herdings Vw. 12	O14	46
Hereford St. 1	L11	35
Hereward Rd. 5	L 6	13
Herewards Rd. 8	M15	45
Hermitage Rd., Roth. 61	O 4	14
Hermitage St. 2	K11	34
Heron Mt. 2	N11	36
Herries Av. 5	L 7	23
Herries Dr. 5	L 7	23
Herries Pl. 5	L 7	23
Herries Rd. 5 & 6	J 7	22
Herries Rd. S. 6	J 7	22
Herringthorpe Av., Roth. 65	U 6	17
Herringthorpe Gro., Roth. 65	V 6	18
Herringthorpe Valley Rd., Roth. 60 & 65	V 4	18
Herrinthorpe La., Roth. 65	V 5	18
Herschell Rd. 7	K12	34
Hesley Grange 61	P 3	5
Hesley Rd. 5	N 4	14
Hesley Ter. 5	N 4	14
Hessey St. 13	Q13	47
Hessle Rd. 6	H 7	21
Hibberd Rd. 6	H 8	21
Hibberd Rd. 6	H 8	21
Hickmott Rd. 11	J12	34
Hicks La. 3	L10	35
Hicks St. 3	K 9	22
Hides St. 9	O 8	24
Higgitt Rd. 9	O 8	24
Janson St.		

Entry	Ref
High Ct. 1	L10 35
High St.	
High Field La. 13	R10 38
High Gate 9	Q 7 25
High Greave 5	M 4 13
High Greave Pl., Roth. 65	V 4 18
High Greave Rd., Roth. 65	V 4 18
High Hazels Clo. 9	P10 37
High Hazels Cres., Cat. 60	S 9 26
High Hazels Mead 9	P10 37
High House Rd. 6	J 8 22
High House Ter. 6	J 8 22
High La. 12	Q15 47
High Matlock Av. 6	F 9 20
High Matlock Rd., Stan. 6	F 8 20
High St. 1	L10 35
High St., Btn. 19	U14 49
High St., Dore 17	F16 52
High St., Eccl. 30	L 4 13
High St., Eck. 31	S18 58
High St., Kimb. 61	Q 4 15
High St., Mosb. 19	S16 58
High St., Raw. 62	T 2 7
High St., Roth. 60	S 5 16
High St., Swall. 31	U12 39
High St., Whis. 60	U 7 27
High Storrs Clo. 11	G13 43
High Storrs Cres. 11	G12 33
High Storrs Dr. 11	G13 43
High Storrs Rd. 11	G12 33
High Storrs Ri. 11	H12 33
High Street La. 2	M10 35
High Trees 17	F16 52
High Wray Clo. 11	H14 43
Highcliffe Dr. 11	G12 33
Highcliffe Dr., Ought. 30	F 5 10
Highcliffe Pl. 11	G13 43
Highcliffe Rd. 11	G12 33
Highfield Pl. 2	L12 35
Highfield Rd., Roth. 61	S 3 6
Highfield Ri., Stan. 6	E 9 20
Highgreave Av. 5	L 4 13
Highnam Crescent Rd. 10	J10 34
Highton St. 6	J 9 22
Hill Clo., Roth. 65	V 6 18
Hill Clo., Stan. 6	F 9 20
Hill Crest Rd., Roth. 65	U 4 17
Hill Side 19	S16 58
Hill St. 2	K11 34
Hill St. 9	P 6 15
Hill Top Clo., Brin. 60	R 7 26
Hill Top Clo., Roth. 61	P 5 15
Hill Top Dr. 30	F 4 10
Hill Top La., Dal.M. 65	X 5 19
Hill Top La., Roth. 61	P 5 15
Hill Top Rd., Gren. 30	J 4 12
Hill Top Ri. 30	J 4 12
Hill Turrets Clo. 11	G14 43
Hill View Rd., Roth. 61	P 4 15
Hillcote Av. 10	F11 32
Hillcote Clo. 10	F11 32
Hillcote Dr. 10	F11 32
Hillfoot Bridge 3	K 9 22
Hillfoot Rd. 17	F17 52
Hillfoot Rd. 3	K 9 22
Neepsend La.	
Hillsborough Pl. 6	J 8 22
Taplin Rd.	
Hillsborough Rd. 6	J 8 22
Hillside Av. 5	L 5 13
Hillside, Whis. 60	U 7 27
Hilltop Cres. 19	S15 48
Hilton Dr., Eccl. 30	L 4 13
Hind Rd., Whis. 60	V 7 28
Hinde House Cres. 4	N 7 24
Hinde House Croft 4	N 7 24
Hinde House La. 4	M 7 23
Hinde St. 4	N 7 24
Hinde Wood Clo. 4	N 7 24
Hirst Common La. 6	H 5 11
Hirst Dr., Roth. 65	V 4 18
Hobart St. 11	K12 34
Hobson Av. 6	K 8 22
Hobson Pl. 6	K 8 22
Hobson Av.	
Hodgson St. 3	K11 34
Holberry Clo. 10	K11 34
Holberry Gdns. 10	K11 34
Holbrook Av., Mosb. 19	T16 59
Holbrook Dr. 13	O12 36
Holbrook Grn. 19	U15 49
Holbrook Rd. 13	O12 36
Holbrook Ri. 19	U15 49
Holdings Rd. 2	M11 35
Holgate Av. 5	K 5 12
Holgate Cres. 5	L 5 13
Holgate Dr. 5	L 5 13
Holgate Rd. 5	L 5 13
Holkham Ri. 11	G15 43
Holland Pl. 2	L12 35
Holland Rd. 2	L12 35
Holland St. 1	K10 34
Hollin Rd., Ought. 30	F 5 10
Hollindale Dr. 12	P13 47
Holling Moor La., Wick. 66	X 6 19
Hollings La., Thry. 65	W 3 8
Hollins Clo. 6	G 9 21
Hollins Dr. 6	G 9 21
Hollins La. 6	G 9 21
Hollinsend Av. 12	P13 47
Hollinsend Pl. 12	P13 47
Hollinsend Rd. 12	O14 46
Hollis Cft. 1	K10 34
Hollow Gate, Whis. 60	U 7 27
Hollow La., Mosb. 19	T17 59
Hollowgate, Roth. 60	T 5 17
Holly Cres., Bram. 66	Y 5 19
Holly Gdns. 12	P13 47
Holly House La. 30	H 4 11
Holly La. 1	L10 35
West St.	
Holly Mt., Wick. 66	Y 6 19
Holly St. 1	L10 35
Holly Ter., Aug. 31	U12 39
Hollybank Av. 12	P13 47
Hollybank Clo. 12	P13 47
Hollybank Cres. 12	P13 47
Hollybank Dr. 12	P13 47
Hollybank Rd. 12	P13 47
Hollybank Way 12	P13 47
Hollybush St., Raw. 62	T 2 7
Hollythorpe Cres. 8	L14 45
Hollythorpe Rd. 8	L14 45
Hollythorpe Ri. 8	L14 45
Holm Oak Way 6	F 8 20
Acorn Dr.	
Holme Clo. 6	J 8 22
Holme La. 6	H 8 21
Holme La., Gren. 30	J 4 12
Holme Way 6	H 8 21
Holmes Cres., Tree. 60	T10 39
Station Rd.	
Holmes La., Roth. 61	R 5 16
Holmes Rd., Bram. 66	Y 6 19
Holmes, The, Roth. 61	R 5 16
Holmesdale Clo., C.A. 18	M18 55
Holmesdale Rd., C.A. 18	L18 55
Holmflatt St., Raw. 62	T 2 7
Holmflatt, Raw. 62	T 2 7
Holmhirst Clo. 8	K14 44
Holmhirst Dr. 8	K14 44
Holmhirst Rd. 8	K14 44
Holmhirst Way 8	K14 44
Holmley Bank, Dron. 18	L18 55
Holmley La., Dron. 18	L18 55
Holmley Ter., Dron. 18	L18 55
Holmsfield Rd., Ought. 30	F 4 10
Holmshaw Dr. 13	Q12 37
Holmshaw Gro. 13	Q12 37
Holtwood Rd. 4	L 8 23
Holy Grn. 1	L11 35
Holyoake Av. 13	Q11 37
Holyrood Ri., Bram. 66	Y 5 19
Holywell Clo., Raw. 62	U 1 7
Holywell Rd. 4 & 9	N 7 24
Homes Cres., Tree. 60	T10 39
Station Rd.	
Homestead Clo. 5	M 5 13
Homestead Dr., Brin. 60	R 7 26
Homestead Rd. 5	M 5 13
Honeysuckle Rd. 5	N 6 14
Hoober Av. 11	G13 43
Hoober Rd. 11	H13 43
Hoodfield Vw., Raw. 62	U 1 7
Hoole La. 10	J11 34
Crookes Rd.	
Hoole Rd. 10	J10 34
Hoole St. 6	J 9 22
Hooley Rd. 13	S13 48
Hope Rd., Ought. 30	G 5 11
Hope Sq. 9	N 8 24
Hope St. 3	K10 34
Hope St., Roth. 60	S 4 16
Hopedale Rd. 12	P14 47
Hopefield Av. 12	P14 47
Hopwood La., Stan. 6	E10 32
Horace St., Roth. 60	T 5 17
Horam Rd. 6	J 9 22
Horndean Rd. 5	M 7 23
Horner Rd. 7	K12 34
Horninglow Clo. 5	M 6 13
Horninglow Mt. 5	M 6 13
Horninglow Rd. 5	M 6 13
Horse Croft La., Ought. 30	E 4 10
Horse Wood Rd. 13	S12 38
Horton Clo. 19	T16 59
Horton Dr. 19	T16 59
Houndkirk Rd. 11	C17 51
Hounsfield Cres., Roth. 65	V 4 18
Hounsfield La. 3	K10 34
Hounsfield Rd.	
Hounsfield Rd. 3	K10 34
Hounsfield Rd., Roth. 65	V 4 18
Houstead Rd. 9	P10 37
Howard Hill 6	J 9 22
Howard Rd.	
Howard Rd. 6	J 9 22
Howard Rd., Bram. 66	Y 5 19
Howard St. 1	L10 35
Howard St., Roth. 60 & 65	S 4 16
Howarth Rd., Brin. 60	S 8 26
Howden Rd. 9	O 8 24
Howdike La., Hoot.R. 65	X 1 9
Howlett Dr., Brin. 60	S 8 26
Hoyland Rd. 3	K 8 22
Hoyle St. 3	K10 34
Hucklow Dr. 5	M 7 23
Hucklow Rd.	
Hucklow Rd. 5	M 7 23
Hudson Rd., Roth. 61	Q 3 5
Hudson Rd., Wd.M. 13	T12 39
Humphrey Rd. 8	K16 54
Hunger Hill La., Whis. 60	V 7 28
Hunger Hill Rd., Whis. 60	U 7 27
Hungerhill Clo., Roth. 61	P 4 11
Hungerhill Rd., Roth. 61	P 3 5
Hunsley St. 4	N 8 24
Hunstone Av. 8	L16 55
Hunter Hill Rd. 11	J12 34
Hunter House Rd. 11	H12 33
Hunter Rd. 6	H 8 21
Hunters Bar 11	J12 34
Hunters Gdns. 6	F 7 20
Archer Gate	
Hunters La. 13	P13 47

Name	Ref		Name	Ref		Name	Ref	
Huntingdon Cres. 11	K12	34	Jaunty Way 12	O14	46	Kenninghall Pl. 2	M12	35
Huntingtower Rd. 11	H12	33	Jedburgh Dr. 9	O 6	14	Kenninghall Rd. 2	M12	35
Huntley Gro. 11	G13	43	Jedburgh St. 9	O 6	14	Kent Av., Raw. 62	T 1	7
Huntley Rd. 11	H13	43	Jeffcock Rd. 9	P10	37	Kent Rd. 8	L13	45
Huntsman Rd. 9	P10	37	*Staniforth Rd.*			Kent Rd., Roth. 61	Q 3	5
Hurl Dr. 12	N13	46	Jeffery Grn. 10	E12	32	Kenwell Dr. 17	H17	53
Hurlfield Av. 12	N13	46	*Harrison La.*			Kenwood Av. 7	K12	34
Hurlfield Ct. 12	O13	46	Jeffery St. 2	L13	45	*Montgomery Rd.*		
Hurlfield Dr. 12	N13	46	Jenkin Av. 9	O 7	24	Kenwood Bank 7	K12	34
Hurlfield Dr., Rav. 65	Y 4	19	Jenkin Clo. 9	O 7	24	Kenwood Park Rd. 7	K12	34
Hurlfield Rd. 12	N13	46	Jenkin Dr. 9	O 7	24	Kenwood Rd. 7	J12	34
Hurlingham Clo. 11	J13	44	Jenkin Rd. 5 & 9	N 6	14	Kenwood Ri., Wick. 66	X 6	19
Hursley Clo. 19	U15	49	Jepson Rd. 5	N 6	14	Kenyon Alley 3	K10	34
Hursley Dr. 19	U15	49	Jericho St. 3	K10	34	*Edward St.*		
Inglewood Av.			Jermyn Av. 12	Q14	47	Kenyon St. 1	K10	34
Hutchinson La. 8	J14	44	Jermyn Clo. 12	Q14	47	Keppel Dr., Sch. 61	O 3	4
Hutchinson Rd. 8	J14	44	Jermyn Cres. 12	Q14	47	Keppel Heights, Sch. 61	O 3	4
Hutchinson Rd., Raw. 62	U 1	7	Jermyn Dr. 12	Q14	47	Keppel Pl. 5	N 5	14
Hutcliffe Dr. 8	J15	44	Jermyn Sq. 12	Q14	47	Keppel Rd. 5	N 5	14
Hutcliffe Wood Rd. 8	J15	44	Jermyn Way 12	Q14	47	Keppel Rd., Sch. 61	O 3	4
Hutton Croft 12	R14	48	Jersey Rd. 2	L12	35	Keppel View Rd., Roth. 61	P 4	15
Hutton Rd., Roth. 61	Q 3	5	*Queens Rd.*			Kerwin Clo. 17	F16	52
Hyacinth Clo. 5	N 6	14	Jessamine Rd. 5	N 6	14	Kerwin Dr. 17	F16	52
Hyacinth Rd. 5	N 6	14	Jessell St. 9	N 9	24	Kerwin Rd. 17	F16	52
Hyde Park Ter. 2	M10	35	Jessop St. 1	L11	35	Kestrel Av., Th.Hes. 61	N 1	4
Hyde Park Wk. 2	M10	35	Jew La. 1	L10	35	Kestrel Grn. 2	N11	36
Ibbotson Rd. 6	J 9	22	*Commerical St.*			*Skye Edge Av.*		
Icknield Way, Brin. 60	S 8	26	Jewitt Rd., Roth. 61	Q 3	5	Keswick Cres., Brin. 60	R 8	26
Idsworth Rd. 5	M 7	23	Jobson Pl. 3	K 9	22	Kettlebridge Rd. 9	O10	36
Ilkley Rd. 5	M 6	13	*Jobson Rd.*			Ketton Av. 8	L14	45
Industry Rd. 9	O 9	24	Jobson Rd. 3	K 9	22	Kew Cres. 12	N15	46
Industry St. 6	J 9	22	John Calvert Rd. 13	S13	48	Keyworth Pl. 13	R13	48
Infield La. 9	P10	37	John St. 2	K11	34	Keyworth Rd. 6	J 7	22
Infirmary Rd. 6	K 9	22	John St., Eck. 31	S18	58	*Middlewood Rd.*		
Infirmary Rd., Raw. 62	U 2	7	John St., Roth. 60	S 5	16	Khartoum Rd. 11	J11	34
Ingelow Av. 5	L 5	13	John Ter., Raw. 62	T 1	7	Kildale Gdns. 19	S16	58
Ingfield Av. 9	Q 7	25	John Ward St. 13	S12	38	Kiln Rd. 61	Q 3	5
Inglewood Av. 19	U15	49	Johnson La. 1	L 9	23	Kilner Way 6	J 6	12
Inglewood Ct. 19	U15	49	*Nursery St.*			Kilnhurst La., Hoot.R. 65	X 1	9
Ingram Cro. 2	M11	35	Johnson St. 3	L 9	23	Kilnhurst Rd., Raw. 62	U 1	7
Ingram Rd. 2	M11	35	Joiner La. 3	L 9	23	Kilton Hill 3	L 9	23
Ingshead Av., Raw. 62	T 1	7	*Nursery St.*			Kilton Pl. 3	L 9	23
Inkersall Dr., Mosb. 19	T16	59	Joiner St. 3	L10	35	*Andover St.*		
Ironside Clo. 14	M14	45	Jordan Cres., Roth. 61	Q 5	15	Kilvington Av. 13	O12	36
Ironside Pl. 14	N14	46	Jordanthorpe Parkway 8	L17	55	Kilvington Cres. 13	O12	36
Ironside Rd. 14	M14	45	Joseph St., Roth. 60	S 4	16	Kilvington Rd. 13	O12	36
Ironside Wk. 14	M15	45	Josephine Rd., Roth. 61	R 5	16	Kimberley St. 9	N 9	24
Irving St. 9	P10	37	Joshua Rd. 7	K12	34	Kimberworth Park Rd., Roth. 61	P 3	5
Islay St. 10	H10	33	Jowitt Rd. 11	J13	44	Kimberworth Rd., Roth. 61	Q 4	15
Forres Rd.			Jubb Clo., Roth. 65	V 6	18	King Ecgbert Rd. 17	G17	53
Ivanhoe Rd. 6	H 9	21	Jubilee Rd. 9	O 9	24	King James St. 6	J 9	22
Ivanhoe Rd. 9	P10	37	Jubilee St., Roth. 60	S 6	16	King St. 3	L10	35
Irving St.			Julian Rd. 9	O 6	14	Kingfield Rd. 11	J12	34
Ivanhoe Rd., Thur. 66	Y 9	29	Julian Way 9	O 6	14	Kingfisher Ri., Th.Hes. 61	N 1	4
Ivy Cottage La. 11	F13	42	Jumble Hole La., Th.Hes. 61	N 3	4	Kings Rd., Eck. 31	T18	59
Ivy Farm Croft, Dal.M. 65	V 3	8	Jumble Rd. 11	D15	41	Kings Way, Roth. 60	U 7	27
Ivy Hall Rd. 5	N 4	14	Junction Rd. 11	J12	34	Kingsforth La., Wick. 66	Y 7	29
Ivy Park Rd. 10	G11	33	Junction Rd., Wood. 13	S12	38	Kingsforth La., Thur. 66	Y 8	29
Jackey La. 30	E 4	10	Junction Ter. 13	T12	39	Kingslake St. 9	O 8	24
Coldwell Hill			June Rd. 13	S12	38	Kingsley Park Av. 7	H14	43
Jackson Cres., Raw. 62	S 1	6	Katherine Rd., Thur. 66	Y 8	29	Kingsley Park Gro. 11	H14	43
Jacobs Clo. 5	N 6	14	Kaye Pl. 10	J10	34	Kingston St. 4	M 8	23
Jacobs Dr. 5	N 6	14	*Barber Rd.*			Kingswood Av. 19	R15	48
Jamaica St. 4	M 8	23	Kearsley Rd. 2	L12	35	*Deanhead Dr.*		
James Andrew Clo. 8	K16	54	Keats Rd. 6	J 5	12	Kingswood Cft. 19	R15	48
James Andrew Cres. 8	K16	54	Keetons Hill 2	K11	34	Kingswood Clo. 19	R15	48
James Andrew Croft 8	K16	54	*London Rd.*			Kingswood Gro. 19	R15	39
James St. 9	P10	37	Keir Pl., Raw. 62	U 1	7	Kinharvie Rd. 5	K 6	12
James St., Roth. 60	S 5	16	Kelham Island 3	L 9	23	Kinnaird Av. 5	M 5	13
Janson St. 9	O 8	24	*Alma St.*			Kinnaird St. 5	M 5	13
Jardine Clo. 9	O 6	14	Kelvin Flats 6	K 9	22	Kinnaird Rd. 5	M 5	13
Jardine St. 9	O 6	14	Kelvin St., Dal.M. 65	V 3	8	Kipling Rd. 6	J 8	22
Jarrow Rd. 11	J12	34	Kenbourne Gro. 7	K12	34	Kirby Clo. 9	P10	37
Jasmine Av. 19	T14	49	Kenbourne Rd. 7	K12	34	Kirk Edge Av. 30	F 6	10
Jaunty Av. 12	P14	47	Kendal Pl. 6	H 8	21	Kirk Edge Dr. 30	F 6	10
Jaunty Clo. 12	O14	46	*Kendal Rd.*			Kirk Edge Rd. 6 & 30	E 5	10
Jaunty Cres. 12	P14	47	Kendal Rd. 6	H 8	21	Kirk St. 4	M 9	23
Jaunty Dr. 12	O14	46	Kenilworth Pl. 11	J12	34			
Jaunty La. 12	O13	46	*Ecclesall Rd.*					
Jaunty Mt. 12	P14	47	Kennedy Rd. 8	K15	44			
Jaunty Pl. 12	O14	46	Kenninghall Clo. 2	M12	35			
Jaunty Rd. 12	P14	47	Kenninghall Dr. 2	M12	35			
Jaunty Vw. 12	P14	47	Kenninghall Mt. 2	M12	35			

Kirkbridge Rd. 9 — O 8 24
Kirkby Av. 12 — O14 46
Kirkby Dr. 12 — O14 46
Kirkby Rd. 12 — O14 46
Kirkby Vw. 12 — O14 46
Kirkby Way 12 — O14 46
Kirkdale Cres. 13 — R11 38
  Retford Rd.
Kirkdale Dr. 13 — R11 38
Kirklands, Raw. 62 — T 1 7
Kirkstall Clo., — R 7 26
  Brin. 60
Kirkstall Rd. 11 — J12 34
Kirkstead Rd., — O 4 14
  Roth. 61
Kirkstone Rd. 6 — J 8 22
Kirton Rd. 4 — M 8 23
Knab Cft. 7 — J13 44
Knab Clo. 11 — J13 44
Knab Rd. 11 — J13 44
Knab Ri. 7 — J13 44
Knapton Av., Raw. 62 — T 1 7
Knaresborough Rd. 7 — J14 44
Knoll, The, Dron. 18 — M18 55
Knowle Clo., Stan. 6 — F 9 20
Knowle Croft 11 — H13 43
Knowle La. 11 — G13 43
Knowle Rd. 5 — L 5 13
Knowle Top, Mosb. 19 — T16 59
Knutton Cres. 5 — K 5 12
Knutton Rd. 5 — K 5 12
Knutton Ri. 5 — K 4 12
Kyle Clo. 5 — K 6 12
Kyle Cres. 5 — K 6 12
Laburnum Av., Bram. 66 — X 5 19
Ladies Spring Dr. 17 — H16 53
Ladies Spring Gro. 17 — H16 53
Lady Idas Dr., Eck. 31 — T18 59
Lady Oak Rd., Roth. 65 — V 4 18
Ladybank Rd. 19 — S17 58
Ladys Bridge 3 — L10 35
  Wicker
Ladysmith Av. 7 — J13 44
Laird Av. 6 — H 7 21
Laird Dr. 6 — H 7 21
Laird Rd. 6 — G 7 21
Lamb Dr. 5 — J 6 12
Lamb Rd. 5 — J 6 12
Lambcroft La. 13 — S13 48
Lambert St. 3 — L10 35
Lambhill Clo. 13 — P12 37
Lancaster St. 3 — K 9 22
  Ball St.
Lancing Rd. 2 — L12 35
Landseer Clo. 14 — N15 46
Landseer Ct., Bram. 66 — X 5 19
Landseer Dr. 14 — N15 46
Landseer Pl. 14 — N15 46
Landseer Wk. 14 — N15 46
Lane End Rd., Roth. 60 — U 7 27
Lane Head 30 — H 4 11
Lane Head Rd. 17 — F18 52
Lanes, The, Roth. 65 — U 4 17
Langdale Dr., C.A. 18 — M18 55
Langdale Rd. 8 — K13 44
Langdon St. 11 — K12 34
Langley Clo., Roth. 65 — V 4 18
Langley St. 9 — P10 37
Langsett Av. 6 — H 7 21
Langsett Clo. 6 — J 8 22
Langsett Cres. 6 — J 8 22
Langsett Gro. 6 — J 9 22
Langsett Rd. 6 — J 8 22
Langsett Rd. N., — F 4 10
  Ought. 30
Langsett Rd. S., — F 4 10
  Ought. 30
Langsett Ri. 6 — J 8 22
Langsett Wk. 6 — J 8 22
  Langsett Cres.
Lansbury Pl., Raw. 62 — V 1 8
Lansbury Rd., Eck. 31 — S18 58
Lansdowne Rd. 11 — K11 34
Lapwater Rd., Roth. 61 — O 2 5

Lapwater Wk., Roth. 61 — Q 2 5
Lapwing Vale, — O 1 4
  Th.Hes. 61
Larch Av., Wick. 66 — X 5 19
Larch Hill 9 — Q10 37
Lark St. 6 — H 9 21
Latham Sq. 11 — G13 43
Lathkill Clo. 13 — P12 37
Lathkill Rd. 13 — P12 37
Lauder St. 4 — M 7 23
  Willoughby St.
Laudesdale Rd., — V 4 18
  Roth. 65
Laughton Rd. 9 — O 7 24
Launce Rd. 5 — K 6 12
Laurel Av., Bram. 66 — Y 5 19
Laverack St. 13 — Q11 37
Laverdene Av. 17 — G18 53
Laverdene Clo. 17 — G18 53
Laverdene Dr. 17 — G18 53
Laverdene Rd. 17 — G18 53
Laverdene Way 17 — G18 53
Laverock Way 5 — M 5 13
Lavinia Rd., Gren. 30 — K 4 12
Lawn, The, Dron. 18 — L18 55
Lawns, The 11 — H13 43
Lawrence Clo., Bram. 66 — X 5 19
Lawrence St. 9 — N 9 24
Lawson Rd. 10 — H10 33
Lawton La., Roth. 60 — T 6 17
Lawton Ter. 6 — H 8 21
  Hawthorn Rd.
Laxey Rd. 6 — G 9 21
Lea, The 19 — S15 48
Leadbeater Dr. 12 — O14 46
Leadbeater Rd. 12 — O14 46
Leader Ct. 6 — H 7 21
Leader Rd. 6 — H 7 21
Leadmill Rd. 1 & 2 — L11 35
Leadmill St. 1 — L11 35
Leake Rd. 6 — J 7 22
Leamington St. 10 — J10 34
Lease Gate Rd., — U 7 27
  Whis. 60
Leaton Clo., Lox. 6 — F 7 20
Leavygreave 3 — K10 34
  Hounsfield Rd.
Leavygreave Rd. 3 — K10 34
Leawood Pl. 6 — F 9 20
Ledsham Rd., Roth. 60 — U 6 17
Ledstone Rd. 8 — K14 44
Lee Croft 1 — L10 35
Lee Rd., Lox. 6 — F 7 20
Leedham Clo. 5 — N 6 14
Leedham Rd. 5 — N 6 14
Leedham Rd., Roth. 65 — V 6 18
Leeds Rd. 9 — O 9 24
Lees Hall Av. 8 — L13 45
Lees Hall Pl. 8 — L13 45
Lees Hall Rd. 8 — L14 45
Lees Nook 8 — L14 45
Leicester Wk. 3 — K10 34
Leigh St. 9 — O 8 24
Leighton Dr. 14 — N14 46
Leighton Pl. 14 — N14 46
Leighton Rd. 14 — N14 46
Lemont Rd. 17 — G18 53
Lennox Rd. 6 — H 7 21
Lenton St. 2 — L11 35
Leonard Clo. 2 — O12 36
Leopold St. 1 — L10 35
Leppings La. 6 — J 7 22
Lescar La. 11 — J12 34
Leslie Rd. 6 — H 7 21
Letard Dr., Brin. 60 — S 7 26
Leverton Dr. 11 — K11 34
Leverton Gdns. 11 — K11 34
Leverton St. 2 — K11 34
  London Rd.
Leverton Way, Dal.M. 65 — W 3 8
  Brierley Rd.
Leveson St. 4 — M 9 23
Lewis Rd. 13 — P12 37
Leybourne Rd., Roth. 61 — Q 3 5

Leyburn Dr., Aug. 31 — U12 39
Leyburn Rd. 8 — K13 44
Leyfield Rd. 17 — F16 52
Liberty Clo. 6 — G 9 21
Liberty Dr. 6 — G 9 21
Liberty Hill 6 — G 9 21
Liberty Pl. 6 — G 9 21
Liberty Rd. 6 — G 9 21
Library Clo., Roth. 61 — R 2 6
Lichford Rd. 2 — M13 45
Lidget La., Bram. 66 — Y 5 19
Lifford St. 9 — Q 6 15
Lightwood La. 8 — N15 46
Lightwood La., — Q18 57
  Marsh. 31
Lilac Gro., Bram. 66 — Y 5 19
Lilac Rd. 5 — N 6 14
Lilac Rd., Btn. 19 — T14 49
Lilian St. S., Roth. 60 — T 5 17
Lilian St., Roth. 60 — T 5 17
Limb La. 17 — F16 52
Limbrick Clo. 6 — J 8 22
Limbrick Rd. 6 — J 8 22
Lime Clo., Rav. 65 — Y 3 9
Lime St. 6 — K 9 22
Lime St., Btn. 19 — T14 49
Limegrove, Roth. 60 — U 6 17
Limestone Cottage La. 6 — H 6 11
Limetree Cres., Raw. 62 — U 1 7
Limpsfield Rd. 9 — O 7 24
Linaker Rd. 6 — H 9 21
Linburn Rd. 8 — K15 44
Lincoln St. 9 — O 7 24
Lincoln St., Roth. 60 — S 4 16
Linden Av. 8 — K15 44
Linden Av., Bram. 66 — Y 5 19
Linden Av., Dron. 18 — L18 55
Lindley Rd. 5 — M 7 23
Lindley St., Roth. 65 — T 4 17
Lindsay Av. 5 — L 6 13
Lindsay Clo. 5 — L 5 13
Lindsay Cres. 5 — L 5 13
Lindsay Dr. 5 — L 5 13
Lindsay Rd. 5 — L 5 13
Lindum Dr., Wick. 66 — Y 6 19
Lindum Ter., Roth. 65 — T 5 17
Lingard La., Wor. 30 — F 5 10
Lingfoot Av. 8 — L17 55
Lingfoot Clo. 8 — L17 55
Lingfoot Cres. 8 — L17 55
Lingfoot Dr. 8 — M17 55
Lingfoot Pl. 8 — L17 55
Lingfoot Wk. 8 — L17 55
Lings Houses, Wick. 66 — Y 6 19
Lings La., Wick. 66 — Y 6 19
Link Rd., Thry. 65 — X 3 9
Link, The 10 — H10 33
Linley La. 12 — P13 47
Linnet Mt., Th. Hes. 61 — N 1 4
Linscott Rd. 8 — K15 44
Lisle Rd., Roth. 60 — U 6 17
Lismore Rd. 8 — L13 45
Lister Av. 12 — O14 46
Lister Clo. 12 — O14 46
Lister Cres. 12 — O14 46
Lister Dr. 12 — O14 46
Lister La. 3 — K 9 22
  Malinda St.
Lister Pl. 12 — O14 46
Lister Rd. 6 — J 9 22
Lister St. 9 — P10 37
  Station Rd.
Lister St., Roth. 65 — T 5 17
Lister Way 12 — O14 46
Little Attercliffe 9 — O 9 24
Little Common La. 11 — G14 43
Little Common La., — P 4 15
  Roth. 61
Little Common La., — W 7 28
  Whis. 60
Little John Copse 6 — F 8 20
Little La. 12 — O13 46
Little La. 4 — N 7 24
  Upwell St.

Little La., Sch. 61	O 2	4
Little La., Th.Hes. 61	N 1	4
Little London Pl. 8	K13	44
Little London Rd. 8	K13	44
Little Matlock Gdns. 6	F 9	20
Little Matlock Way 6	F 9	20
High Matlock Av.		
Little Norton Av. 8	L16	55
Little Norton Dr. 8	L16	55
Little Norton La. 8	L16	55
Little Norton Way 8	L16	55
Littledale Rd. 9	P11	37
Littlemoor, Eck. 31	T18	59
Littlewood Dr. 12	O14	46
Littlewood La. 12	N14	46
Littlewood Rd. 12	O14	46
Liverick Dr., Raw. 62	V 1	8
Liverpool Pl. 9	N 8	24
Liverpool St.		
Liverpool St. 9	N 8	24
Livesey St. 6	J 7	22
Livingstone Rd. 9	N 9	29
Birch Rd.		
Llewellyn St., Roth. 60	S 5	16
Lloyd St. 4	M 7	23
Lloyd St., Raw. 62	T 2	7
Loakfield Dr. 5	K 4	12
Loakwood Av. 5	K 4	12
Lock House Rd. 9	O 7	24
Attercliffe Common		
Lock La. 9	Q 6	15
Lock Rd. 13	R11	38
Lock St. 6	K 9	22
Locksley Dr., Thur. 66	Y 9	29
Lockwood Clo., Roth. 65	V 4	18
Lockwood Rd., Roth. 65	V 4	18
Lodge La. 10	E11	32
Lodge La., Th.Hes. 61	N 2	4
Lodge Moor Rd. 10	E12	32
Lofthouse Rd. 6	J 7	22
Logan Rd. 9	P10	37
Lomas Clo., Stan. 6	F 8	20
Lomas Lea, Stan. 6	E 8	20
London Rd. 2	K11	34
London Way, Th.Hes. 61	N 2	4
Long Av. 6	C10	31
Long Causeway 10	A13	40
Long Causeway 10	E11	32
Redmires Rd.		
Long Croft Rd.,	J18	54
D.Wd. 18		
Long La. 10	G10	33
Long La., Lox. 6	F 7	20
Long La., Ought. 30	F 4	10
Long La., Stan. 6	F 9	20
Long La., Tree. 60	T 9	27
Long La., Whis. 60	U 8	27
Long La., Wor. 30	F 6	10
Long Line 11	E15	42
Long Steps 2	M10	35
Bernard St.		
Long Wk. 10	H10	33
Longacre Clo. 19	U15	49
Longacre Way 19	U16	59
Longfellow Dr.,	U 5	17
Roth. 65		
Longfield Rd. 10	H 9	21
Longford Clo. 17	H17	53
Longford Cres. 17	H17	53
Longford Dr. 17	G18	53
Longford Rd. 17	H17	53
Longford Spinney 17	G18	53
Longford Rd.		
Longlands Dr., Thry. 65	X 2	9
Longley Av. W. 5	K 7	22
Longley Clo. 5	L 7	23
Longley Cres. 5	L 6	13
Longley Dr. 5	L 7	23
Longley Hall Gro. 5	L 7	23
Longley Hall Rd. 5	L 7	23
Longley Hall Ri. 5	L 7	23
Longley Hall Way 5	L 7	23
Longley La. 5	L 7	23
Longstone Cres. 12	P14	47

Lonsdale Rd. 6	J 8	22
Loosemore Dr. 12	N13	46
Lopham St. 3	L 9	23
Lord St., Roth. 65	U 4	17
Louden Rd., Sch. 61	O 3	4
Lound Rd. 9	P10	37
Louth Rd. 11	H12	33
Love La. 3	L10	35
Love St. 3	L10	35
Lovell St. 4	M 9	23
Lovetot Rd. 9	N 9	24
Lovetot Rd., Roth. 61	Q 3	5
Low Coach Rd., Roth. 61	S 2	6
Low La., Roth. 61	R 4	16
Low Matlock La., Lox. 6	G 8	21
Low Rd. 6	H 9	21
Low Rd., Ought. 30	F 4	10
Lowburn Rd. 13	P12	37
Lowedges Cres. 8	K17	54
Lowedges Dr. 8	K17	54
Lowedges Pl. 8	L17	55
Lowedges Rd. 8	K17	54
Lowfield Av., Roth. 61	S 2	6
Lowfield Clo., Ridg. 12	Q15	47
Lowhouse Rd. 5	N 4	14
Lowther Rd. 6	J 7	22
Loxley New Rd. 6	H 8	21
Loxley Rd., Lox. 6	E 7	20
Loxley View Rd. 10	H 9	21
Loy Clo., Roth. 61	R 2	6
Lucas St. 4	M 8	23
Luke La. 6	G 7	21
Lumb La., Ought. 30	E 4	10
Lumley St. 4 & 9	M10	35
Luna Croft 12	N15	46
Lund Rd., Wor. 30	F 5	10
Lundwood Clo. 19	S15	39
Lundwood Dr. 19	S15	48
Lundwood Gro. 19	S15	48
Lupton Cres. 8	K17	54
Lupton Dr. 8	K17	54
Lupton Rd. 8	K17	54
Lupton Wk. 8	L17	55
Lydgate Hall Cres. 10	H10	33
Lydgate La. 10	H10	33
Lyme St., Roth. 60	S 5	16
Lyminster Rd. 6	J 5	12
Lymister Av., Roth. 60	T 7	27
Lyndhurst Clo. 11	J13	44
Lyndhurst Grn. 11	J12	34
Lyndhurst Rd. 11	J12	34
Lynmouth Rd. 7	K13	44
Lynn Pl. 9	O 8	24
Lynton Av., Roth. 60	U 6	17
Lynton Rd. 11	J12	34
Lyons Clo. 4	M 8	23
Lyons Rd.		
Lyons Rd. 4	M 8	23
Lyons St. 4	M 8	23
Lytton Av. 5	K 5	12
Lytton Cres. 5	K 5	12
Lytton Dr. 5	K 5	12
Lytton Rd. 5	K 5	12
Mabel St., Roth. 60	T 5	17
Machon Bank 7	K13	44
Machon Bank Rd. 7	J12	34
Mackenzie Cres. 10	K11	34
Mackenzie St. 11	K12	34
Madehurst Gdns. 2	L12	35
Madehurst Rd. 2	L12	35
Madehurst Ri. 2	L12	35
Madehurst Vw. 2	L12	35
Magna Clo., Bram. 66	X 5	19
Magna Cres., Wick. 66	X 5	19
Magna La., Dal.M. 65	Y 3	8
Magpie Gro. 2	N11	36
Skye Edge Av.		
Mahon Av., Raw. 62	T 1	7
Maidstone Rd. 6	J 6	12
Main Av. 17	G18	53
Main Rd. 12	Q16	57
Main Rd. 9	P10	37
Main St. 12	R14	48
Main St., Bram. 66	Y 5	19

Main St., Cat. 60	S 9	26
Main St., Greas. 61	S 2	6
Main St., Gren. 30	J 4	12
Main St., Raw. 62	U 1	7
Main St., Roth. 60	S 5	16
Main St., Swall. 31	U12	39
Malin Rd. 6	H 8	21
Malin Rd., Roth. 65	V 4	18
Malinda St. 3	K 9	22
Mallard Clo.,	O 1	4
Th.Hes. 61		
Mallory Rd., Roth. 65	V 4	18
Maltby St. 9	O 8	24
Malting La. 4	M 9	23
Effingham St.		
Maltkiln St., Roth. 60	S 5	16
Malton St. 4	M 8	23
Maltravers Clo. 2	N11	36
Maltravers Cres. 2	M10	35
Maltravers Pl. 2	N10	36
Maltravers Rd. 2	M10	35
Maltravers St. 4	M10	35
Maltravers Ter. 2	N11	36
Maltravers Way 2	N10	36
Malvern Rd. 9	O 9	24
Manchester Rd. 10	E10	32
Manchester Rd. 6	A10	30
Mandeville St. 9	P 9	25
Manell Ter. 3	K 9	22
Jobson Rd.		
Mangham Way 61	S 3	6
Manners St. 3	K 9	22
Rutland Rd.		
Mannheim Rd. 10	H 9	21
Northfield Rd.		
Manor App., Roth. 61	Q 4	15
Manor Cres., Brin. 60	R 8	26
Manor Fields, Roth. 61	Q 4	15
Manor House Rd.,	Q 4	15
Roth. 61		
Manor La. 2	N11	36
Manor Laithe Rd. 2	M11	35
Manor Oaks Clo. 2	N10	36
Manor Oaks Pl. 2	N11	36
Manor Oaks Rd. 2	M10	35
Manor Park Av. 2	N11	36
Manor Park Centre 2	N11	36
Manor Park Clo. 2	N11	36
Manor Park Cres. 2	N11	36
Manor Park Ct. 2	N11	36
Manor Park Dr. 2	N11	36
Manor Park Pl. 2	N11	36
Manor Park Rd. 2	N11	36
Manor Park Ri. 2	N11	36
Manor Park Way 2	N11	36
Manor Pl., Raw. 62	U 1	7
Manor Rd., Brin. 60	R 8	26
Manor Vw. 19	T16	59
Manor Way 2	N10	36
Mansel Av. 5	K 5	12
Mansel Cres. 5	J 5	12
Mansel Rd. 5	K 5	12
Mansfield Dr. 12	O13	46
Mansfield Rd. 12	O13	46
Mansfield Rd.,	U12	39
Swall. 31		
Mansfield Rd., Roth. 60	T 5	17
Manton St. 2	L11	35
Manvers Rd. 6	J 8	22
Manvers Rd., Btn. 19	T14	49
Maple Croft Cres. 5	N 6	14
Maple Croft Rd. 5	N 6	14
Maple Dr., Bram. 66	X 5	19
Maple Gro. 9	Q10	37
Maplebeck Dr. 9	Q 7	25
Maplebeck Rd. 9	Q 7	25
Mappin St. 1	K10	34
Mappins Rd., Cat. 60	S 9	26
March Bank, Thry. 65	X 2	9
March Flatts Rd.,	X 3	9
Thry. 65		
March St. 9	O 8	24
Marcham Dr., Btn. 19	U14	49
Marchwood Av. 6	G 9	21

97

98

Name	Grid	Pg
Molloy Pl. 8	L13	45
Molloy St. 8	L13	45
Mona Av. 10	J10	34
Mona Rd. 10	J 9	22
Monckton Rd. 5	N 6	14
Moncrieffe Rd. 7	K13	44
Monks Clo., Roth. 61	P 3	5
Monkwood Rd., Raw. 62	T 1	7
Monmouth St. 3	K10	34
Filey St.		
Mons St. 9	O 7	24
Montagu Rd. 6	J 8	22
Langsett Rd.		
Montague St. 11	K11	34
Monteney Cres. 5	L 4	13
Monteney Rd. 5	L 4	13
Montfort Dr. 3	L 9	23
Montfort St. 3	L 9	23
Montgomery Av. 7	K12	34
Montgomery Dr. 7	K12	34
Montgomery Mt. 7	K13	44
Machon Bank Rd.		
Montgomery Rd. 7	K12	34
Montgomery Terrace Rd. 6	K 9	22
Montrose Rd. 7	J13	44
Moonshine La. 5	K 6	12
Moor Cres. 19	S16	58
Moor End Rd. 10	J10	34
Moor Hall La. 19	R15	48
Moor Valley		
Moor La. N., Rav. 65	Y 3	9
Moor La. S., Rav. 65	Y 4	19
Moor Main Rd., Ridg. 12	Q16	57
Moor Main Rd., Ridg. 12	Q16	57
Moor Oaks Rd. 10	J10	34
Moor Rd., Roth. 65	U 5	17
Moor Valley 12	Q15	47
Moor View Dr. 8	K14	44
Moor View Rd. 8	K15	44
Moor View Ter. 11	G13	43
Trap La.		
Moor, The 1	L11	35
Moorbank Clo. 10	F10	32
Moorbank Ct. 10	F10	32
Moorbank Dr. 10	G10	33
Moorbank Rd. 10	F10	32
Moorcroft Av. 10	E12	32
Moorcroft Clo. 10	E12	32
Moorcroft Dr. 10	E12	32
Moorcroft Rd. 10	E12	32
Moordale Vw., Raw. 62	V 1	8
Moore St. 3	K11	34
Moorfield Gro., Rav. 65	Y 4	19
Moorfields 3	K 9	22
Moorgate Av. 10	J10	34
Moorgate Chase, Roth. 60	T 5	17
Moorgate Gro., Roth. 60	T 6	17
Moorgate La., Roth. 60	T 6	17
Moorgate Rd., Roth. 60	T 5	17
Moorgate St., Roth. 60	S 5	16
Moorgate Ter., Roth. 60	T 6	17
Moorhouse La., Whis. 60	V 7	28
Moorland Pl., Stan. 6	F 9	20
Moorland Vw. 12	O15	46
Moorlands, Wick. 66	W 6	18
Moorside Clo. 19	S16	58
Moorsyde Av. 10	H 9	21
Moorsyde Cres. 10	H 9	21
Moorthorpe Gdns. 19	Q15	47
Moorthorpe Grn., Hack. 12	R15	47
Moorthorpe Way, Hack. 12	R15	47
Moorwood La., Stan. 6	C10	31
Mordaunt Rd. 2	N13	46
Morgan Av. 5	K 6	12
Morgan Clo. 5	K 6	12
Morgan Rd. 5	K 7	22
Morland Clo. 14	N14	46
Morland Dr. 14	N14	46
Morland Pl. 14	N14	46
Morland Rd. 14	N14	46
Morley Rd., Roth. 61	Q 3	5
Morley St. 6	H 8	21
Morley St., Raw. 62	T 2	7
Morpeth St. 3	K10	34
Morpeth St., Roth. 65	T 5	17
Morrall Rd. 5	K 4	12
Mortain Rd., Roth. 60	T 7	27
Morthen La., Thur. 66	W 9	28
Morthen Rd., Wick. 66	Y 6	19
Mortimer St. 1	L11	35
Mortlake Rd. 5	M 7	23
Morton Pl., Gren. 30	J 4	12
Mosborough Hall Dr. Mosb. 19	T17	59
Mosborough Moor, Mosb. 19	R16	58
Mosborough Rd. 13	O12	36
Moseley La. 1	L10	35
Paradise St.		
Moss Clo., Wick. 66	X 6	19
Moss Gro. 12	S14	48
Moss Rd. 17	E18	52
Moss Vw. 19	R17	58
Moss Way 19	S15	48
Mossdale Av. 19	S16	58
Motehall Dr. 2	O11	36
Motehall Pl. 2	O11	36
Motehall Rd. 2	O11	36
Motehall Way 2	O11	36
Motte, The, Roth. 61	Q 4	15
Mount Pleasant Rd. 7	K12	34
Mount Pleasant Rd., Roth. 61	R 4	16
Mount Rd. 3	K 8	22
Mount St. 11	K11	34
Mount St., Roth. 61	R 4	16
Mount View Av. 8	L14	45
Mount View Gdns. 8	L14	45
Mount View Rd. 8	L14	45
Mount, The 10	J11	34
Mountenoy Rd., Roth. 60	S 5	16
Mountford Cft., Tot. 17	G17	53
Mowbray Gdns., Roth. 65	U 4	17
Mowbray Pl., Roth. 65	V 4	18
Mowbray St. 3	L 9	23
Mowbray St., Roth. 65	U 4	17
Mowson Cres., Wor. 30	F 5	10
Mowson Dr., Wor. 30	F 5	10
Mowson La.Wor. 30	F 5	10
Mulberry St. 1	L10	35
Mulehouse Rd. 10	H10	33
Mundella Pl. 8	L14	45
Mungy La., Thry. 65	V 3	8
Munsbrough La., Roth. 61	R 3	6
Munsbrough Ri., Roth. 61	R 2	6
Murdock Rd. 5	K 6	12
Murray Rd. 11	H12	33
Murray Rd., Raw. 62	U 1	7
Murrayfield Dr., Mosb. 19	T17	59
Musgrave Cres. 5	L 7	23
Musgrave Dr. 5	L 7	23
Musgrave Pl. 5	L 7	23
Musgrave Rd. 5	K 7	22
Musgrove Av., Thry. 65	X 3	9
Mushroom La. 3 & 10	J10	34
Muskoka Av. 11	G13	43
Muskoka Dr. 11	G13	43
Myers Clo., Augh. 30	F 4	10
Myers Grove La. 6	G 8	21
Myers La., Wor. 30	E 6	10
Mylnhurst Rd. 11	H13	43
Mylor Rd. 11	H13	43
Myrtle Cres., Wick. 66	Y 5	19
Myrtle Rd. 2	L12	35
Myrtle Springs 12	N13	46
Myton Rd. 9	O10	36
Ribston Rd.		
Nab La. 12	P15	47
Nairn St. 10	P10	37
Napier St. 11	K11	34
Narrow Twitchell, Roth. 60	T 5	17
Narrow Wk. 10	J10	34
Naseby St. 9	O 7	24
Nathan Ct. 19	T15	49
Nathan Dr. 19	T15	49
Nathan Gro. 19	T15	49
Navan Rd. 2	O12	36
Naylor Gro., Ought. 30	F 5	10
Naylor Rd., Ought. 30	F 4	10
Naylor St., Raw. 62	T 2	7
Nearcroft Rd. 61	Q 4	15
Needham Way 7	J13	44
Neepsend La. 3	K 9	22
Neill Rd. 11	J12	34
Nelson Clo., Brin. 60	S 8	26
Nelson Mandela Wk. 2	P11	37
Nelson Rd. 6	G 9	21
Nelson St., Roth. 65	T 5	17
Nesfield Way 5	M 6	13
Nether Av., Gren. 30	J 4	12
Nether Cres., Gren. 30	J 4	12
Nether Edge Rd. 7	K13	44
Nether Shire La. 5	M 4	13
Netherfield La., Raw. 62	T 2	7
Netherfield Rd. 10	H 9	21
Netherfield, Roth. 65	U 4	17
Nethergate, Stan. 6	E 9	20
Nethergreen Rd. 11	G12	33
Nethermoor Dr., Wick. 66	Y 7	29
Nethermoor La., Wick. 66	Y 7	29
Netherthorpe La., Killa. 31	U16	59
Netherthorpe Pl. 3	K 9	22
Netherthorpe Rd. 3	K10	34
Netherthorpe St. 3	K10	34
Dover St.		
Netherthorpe Wk. 3	K 9	22
Netherthorpe Pl.		
Nettleham Rd. 8	K14	44
Neville Clo. 3	L 9	23
Neville Dr. 3	L 9	23
Neville Rd., Roth. 61	Q 3	5
Neville St., Roth. 60	S 4	16
New Cross Dr. 13	R12	38
New Cross Way 13	R13	48
New Cross Wk. 13	R13	48
New Droppingwell Rd., Roth. 61	O 5	14
New Rd., Roth. 61	O 5	14
New St. 1	L10	35
New St. 19	U16	59
Holbrook		
New St., Cat. 60	S 9	26
New St., Hol. 19	U16	59
New St., Raw. 62	T 1	7
New St., Roth. 61	R 2	6
New St., Th.Hes. 61	N 2	4
New Street La. 2	M10	35
Broad St.		
Newbould Cres. 19	U14	49
Newbould La. 10	J11	34
Newburn Dr. 9	Q 7	25
Newburn Rd. 9	P 7	25
Town St.		
Newbury Rd. 10	H10	33
Newcastle St. 1	K10	34
Newent La. 10	H10	33
Newfield Cres. 17	F16	52
Newfield Croft 17	F16	52
Newfield Farm Clo. 7	M13	45
Newfield Green Rd. 2	M13	45
Newfield La. 17	F16	52
Newhall Av., Wick. 66	Y 7	29
Newhall Rd. 9	N 8	24
Newington Rd. 11	J12	34
Newlands Av. 12	O13	46
Newlands Dr. 12	O13	46
Newlands Gro. 12	O13	46
Newlands Rd. 12	O13	46
Newlyn Pl. 8	L14	45

Newlyn Rd. 8	K14	44
Newman Clo. 9	O 6	14
Newman Ct., Roth. 60	U 7	27
Newman Dr. 9	O 6	14
Newman Rd. 9	N 6	14
Newman Rd., Roth. 60	U 7	27
Newmarch St. 9	Q 6	15
Newsham Rd. 8	K13	44
Newstead Av. 12	Q15	47
Newstead Av., Ought. 30	F 4	10
Newstead Clo. 12	Q14	47
Newstead Dr. 12	Q15	47
Newstead Gro. 12	Q14	47
Newstead Pl. 12	Q15	47
Newstead Rd. 12	Q14	47
Newstead Ri. 12	Q15	47
Newstead Way 12	Q15	47
Newton Dr., Roth. 65	U 5	17
Newton Pl., Th.Hes. 61	N 2	4
Newton St., Roth. 65	U 5	17
Niagara Rd. 6	J 6	12
Nichols Rd. 6	H 9	21
Nicholson Pl. 8	L13	45
Nicholson Rd. 8	L13	45
Nidd Rd. 9	O 9	24
Nidd Rd. E. 9	O 9	24
Nidderdale Pl., Bram. 66	Y 5	19
Nidderdale Rd., Roth. 61	Q 2	5
Nightingale Cft., Th.Hes. 61	O 1	4
Nightingale Rd., Gren. 30 *Grenfolds Rd.*	J 4	12
Nile St. 10	J11	34
Nodder Rd. 13	P12	37
Nodder St., Raw. 62	T 2	7
Noehill Pl. 2	O11	36
Noehill Rd. 2	O11	36
Nook End 6 *Stannington Rd.*	F 9	20
Nook La., Stan. 6	F 9	20
Nook, The 10	J10	34
Norborough Rd. 9	Q 7	25
Norbrook Way, Whis. 60	V 7	28
Norfolk Hill, Gren. 30	J 4	12
Norfolk La. 1	L10	35
Norfolk Park Av. 2	M11	35
Norfolk Park Dr. 2	M11	35
Norfolk Park Rd. 2	M11	35
Norfolk Rd. 2	M11	35
Norfolk Row 1	L10	35
Norfolk St. 1	L10	35
Norfolk St., Roth. 65	S 4	16
Norfolk Way, Roth. 60	T 7	27
Norgreave Way, Mosb. 19	T16	59
Norman St. 9	O 8	24
Normancroft Cres. 2	P11	37
Normancroft Ct. 2	O11	36
Normancroft Dr. 2	O11	36
Normancroft Way 2	P11	37
Normandale Av., Lox. 6	G 8	21
Normanton Gdns. 4	M 8	23
Normanton Gro. 13	Q13	47
Normanton Hill 13	P13	47
Normanton Spring Ct. 13	Q13	47
Normanton Spring Rd. 13	Q13	47
Normanville Av., Brin. 60	R 7	26
Norrels Croft, Roth. 60	T 6	17
Norris Rd. 6	H 8	21
Norroy St. 4	M 9	23
North Church St. 1	L10	35
North Cres., Roth. 65	U 4	17
North Field La., Wick. 66	X 5	19
North Greaves Rd., Roth. 61	R 4	16
North Hill Rd. 5	K 6	12
North Pitt St., Roth. 61	Q 5	15
North Pl., Roth. 65	U 4	17
North Quadrant 5	M 6	13
North Rd., Roth. 65	U 4	17
North St. 6	K 9	22
North St., Raw. 62	U 1	7
North St., Roth. 60	S 4	16
Northcote Av. 2	L13	45
Northcote Rd. 2	L13	45
Northern Av. 2	N12	36
Northern Common, D.Wd. 18	H18	53
Northfield Av. 10	H 9	21
Northfield Av., Raw. 62	T 1	7
Northfield Rd. 10	H10	33
Northfield Rd., Roth. 60	S 4	16
Northlands Rd. 5	K 6	12
Northumberland Rd. 10	J10	34
Norton Av. 12 & 14	N15	46
Norton Church Rd. 8	L15	45
Norton Green Clo. 8	M15	45
Norton Hammer La. 8	K14	44
Norton La. 8	L16	55
Norton Lees Clo. 8	L14	45
Norton Lees Cres. 8	L14	45
Norton Lees La. 8	L14	45
Norton Lees Rd. 8	K13	44
Norton Lees Sq. 8	L14	45
Norton Park Av. 8	L16	55
Norton Park Cres. 8	L16	55
Norton Park Dr. 8	L16	55
Norton Park Rd. 8	L16	55
Norton Park Vw. 8	L16	55
Norwich St. 2	L10	35
Norwood Av. 5	L 7	23
Norwood Clo. 5	L 7	23
Norwood Dr. 5	L 7	23
Norwood Grange Dr. 5 *Longley La.*	L 7	23
Norwood Rd. 5	L 7	23
Norwood St., Dal.M. 65	V 3	8
Nottingham Cliff 3	L 9	23
Nottingham Clo., Brin. 60	R 8	26
Nottingham St. 3	L 9	23
Nottingham St., Roth. 65	T 4	17
Nowill Ct. 2 *Tillotson Ri.*	L13	45
Nowill Pl. 2	L13	45
Nunnery Cres., Cat. 60	S 9	26
Nunnery Dr. 2	N10	36
Nunnery Pit Rd. 9 *Woodbourn Rd.*	N10	36
Nunnery Ter. 2	N10	36
Nursery Dr., Cat. 60	S 9	26
Nursery Dr., Eccl. 30	L 4	13
Nursery Gro., Eccl. 30	L 4	13
Nursery La. 3	L 9	23
Nursery St. 3	L 9	23
Nuttall Pl. 2	M10	35
Oak Apple Clo. 6	F 8	20
Oak Bank Ct. 17	G17	53
Oak Clo., Bram. 66	X 5	19
Oak Dale Rd. 7	J13	44
Oak Hill Rd. 7	J13	44
Oak Hill, Roth. 65	U 4	17
Oak Lea, Roth. 61	R 2	6
Oak Pk. 10	H11	33
Oak Rd. 12	O15	46
Oak Rd., Btn. 19	T14	49
Oak St. 8	L12	35
Oak St., Mosb. 19	S16	58
Oak Ter. 2 *View Rd.*	L12	35
Oak Ter., Aug. 31 *Chestnut Rd.*	U12	39
Oak Ter., Raw. 62	T 1	7
Oak Wood Cres., Wor. 30	F 5	10
Oakbank Ct., Tot. 17	G17	53
Oakbrook Rd. 11	G12	33
Oakdale Pl., Roth. 61	Q 5	15
Oakdale Rd., Roth. 61	Q 5	15
Oakdene, C.A.18	M18	55
Oakenwood Rd., Th.Hes. 61	N 1	4
Oakes Grn. 9	N 9	24
Oakes Park Vw. 14	M15	45
Oakes St. 9 *Fife St.*	O 6	14
Oakham Dr. 3	K 9	22
Oakhill Rd., Dron. 18	M18	55
Oakholme Rd. 10	J11	34
Oakland Rd. 6	H 8	21
Oakley Rd. 13	Q11	37
Oaks Fold 5	N 5	14
Oaks Fold Av. 5	N 5	14
Oaks Fold Rd. 5	N 5	14
Oaks La. 5	N 5	14
Oaks La., Roth. 61	P 3	5
Oakwood Av. 5	K 4	12
Oakwood Dr., Roth. 60	U 6	17
Oakwood Gro., Roth. 60	U 6	17
Oakwood Rd. E., Roth. 60	U 6	17
Oakwood Rd. W., Roth. 60	T 6	17
Oakwood, Raw. 62	T 1	7
Oakworth Clo. 19	S17	58
Oakworth Dr. 19	S16	58
Oakworth Gro. 19	S17	58
Oakworth Vw. 19	T17	59
Oates Av., Raw. 62	U 1	7
Oates St., Roth. 61	R 4	16
Occupation La. 12	Q14	47
Occupation La. 6	F 7	20
Ochre Dike Clo., Btn. 19	T15	49
Ochre Dike La. 19	S15	48
Octavia Clo., Brin. 60	S 7	26
Odd Hill La., Dal.M. 65	W 4	18
Odom Ct. 2 *Gleadless Rd.*	L13	45
Ogden Pl. 8 *Meadow Head*	L16	55
Old Field Shutt La., Dal.M. 65	W 4	18
Old Fulwood Rd. 10	F12	33
Old Garden Dr., Roth. 65	U 4	17
Old Gate La., Thry. 65	W 3	8
Old Hall Dr., Bram. 66	Y 5	19
Old Hall Rd. 9	O 8	24
Old Hay Clo. 17	F17	52
Old Hay Gdns. 17	F17	52
Old Hay La. 17	F17	52
Old La., Mosb. 19	T16	59
Old Park Av. 8	J16	54
Old Park Rd. 8	J16	54
Old Retford Rd., Wood. 13	S11	38
Old School La., Cat. 60	S 9	26
Old Sheffield Rd., Roth. 60	S 5	16
Old St. 2	M10	35
Old Wortley Rd., Roth. 61	Q 4	15
Oldale Clo. 13	S13	48
Oldale Ct. 13	S13	48
Oldale Gro. 13	S13	48
Oldfield Av., Stan. 6	F 9	20
Oldfield Clo., Stan. 6	F 9	20
Oldfield Gro., Stan. 6	F 9	20
Oldfield Rd., Roth. 65	V 4	18
Oldfield Rd., Stan. 6	E 9	20
Oldfield Ter., Stan. 6	F 9	20
Oldwell Clo. 7	F18	52
Olive Cres. 12	O15	46
Olive Grove Rd. 2	L12	35
Olive Rd. 19	S16	58
Olive Ter., Lox. 6	F 8	20
Oliver Rd. 7	J14	44
Olivers Dr. 9	P10	37
Olivers Mt. 9	P10	37
Olivet Rd. 8	K14	44
Omdurman St. 9	O 9	24
Onchan Rd. 6	G 9	21

Name	Grid	Page
Onesmoor Bottom, Ought. 30	E 4	10
Onksley La., Stan. 6	C10	31
Onslow Rd. 11	H12	33
Orange Clo., Brin. 60	S 9	26
Brinsworth Rd.		
Orange St. 1	K10	34
Orchard Clo. 5	L 4	13
Orchard Cres. 5	L 4	13
Orchard Flatts Cres., Roth. 61	R 2	6
Orchard La. 1	L10	35
Orchard La., Btn. 19	T14	49
Orchard Pl., Roth. 60	S 5	16
Orchard Rd. 6	J 9	22
Orchard St. 1	L10	35
Orchard St., Ought. 30	F 4	10
Orgreave Clo. 13	R11	38
Orgreave Cres. 13	S11	38
Orgreave Dr. 13	S11	38
Orgreave La. 13	R11	38
Orgreave Pl. 13	R11	38
Orgreave Rd. 13	R11	38
Orgreave Rd., Cat. 60	S10	38
Orgreave Way, Wd.M. 13	S12	38
Orgreave Wk., Wd.M. 13	S12	38
Oriel Rd. 10	F12	32
Ormond Clo. 8	L17	55
Ormond Dr. 8	L16	55
Ormond Rd. 8	L16	55
Ormond Way 8	L16	55
Orpen Dr. 14	N15	46
Orpen Way 14	N15	46
Orphanage Rd. 3	L 8	23
Osbert Rd., Roth. 60	U 6	17
Osberton Pl. 11	J12	34
Osberton St., Dal.M 65	V 3	8
Osberton St., Raw. 62	U 1	7
Osborne Clo. 11	J12	34
Osborne Rd. 11	J12	34
Osgathorpe Cres. 4	M 8	23
Osgathorpe Dr. 4	M 8	23
Osgathorpe Rd. 4	M 8	23
Osmaston Rd. 8	K15	44
Osmund Rd., Eck. 31	R18	58
Osprey Gdns. 2	N11	36
Skye Edge Av.		
Oswestry Rd. 5	M 6	13
Otley Wk. 6	J 9	22
Otter St. 9	N 9	24
Oughtibridge La., Ought. 30	G 4	11
Ouse Rd. 9	O 9	24
Ouseburn Croft 9	O 9	24
Ouseburn Rd. 9	O 9	24
Ouseburn St. 9	O 9	24
Nidd Rd.		
Outram Rd. 2	N11	36
Oval Rd., Roth. 65	U 4	17
Oval, The 5	M 6	13
Overcroft Ri. 17	F18	52
Overdale Gdns. 17	F17	52
Overdale Ri. 17	F17	52
Overend Clo. 14	M14	45
Overend Dr. 14	M14	45
Overend Rd. 14	M14	45
Overend Way 14	M14	45
Oversley St. 9	Q 6	15
Overton Rd. 6	H 7	21
Owen Clo. 6	J 5	12
Owen Pl. 6	J 5	12
Owen Wk. 6	J 5	12
Owler Bar Rd. 17	B17	50
Owler Car La., C.A. 18	N18	56
Owler La. 4	M 7	23
Owlerton Grn. 6	J 8	22
Owlet La. 4	N 7	24
Owlings Pl. 6	H 8	21
Owlings Rd. 6	H 7	21
Owlthorpe Greenway 19	S15	48
Owlthorpe La., Mosb. 19	R16	58
Owlthorpe Ri., Mosb. 19	R16	58
Ox Close Av., Bradw. 17	H17	53
Ox Close Av., Roth. 61	Q 3	5
Oxford Row, Roth. 61	S 2	6
Oxford St. 6	J10	34
Oxford St., Roth. 65	U 4	17
Oxley Gro., Roth. 60	T 6	17
Oxspring Bank 5	J 7	22
Oxted Rd. 9	O 7	24
Paddock Cres. 2	N13	46
Paddock Way, C.A. 18	M18	55
Paddock, The, Thry. 65	X 3	9
Vale Rd.		
Padley Way 5	M 6	13
Page Hall Rd. 4	M 7	23
Paget St. 9	N 8	24
Palgrave Cres. 5	K 6	12
Palgrave Rd. 5	J 6	12
Palm Hollow Clo., Wick. 66	W 6	18
Palm La. 6	J 9	22
Palm St. 6	J 9	22
Palmer Rd. 9	P 9	25
Palmer St. 9	N 9	24
Palmerston Rd. 10	J10	34
Paper Mill Rd. 5	N 4	14
Parade, The 12	O13	46
Newlands Rd.		
Paradise La. 1	L10	35
Paradise Sq. 1	L10	35
Campo La.		
Paradise St. 1	L10	35
Park Av. 10	H12	33
Park Av., Whis. 60	V 7	28
Park Cres. 10	J11	34
Park Cres., Eccl. 30	L 4	13
Park Dr., Swall. 31	U12	39
Park Grange Clo. 2	M12	35
Park Grange Croft 2	M11	35
Park Grange Dr. 2	M12	35
Park Grange Mt. 2	M12	35
Park Grange Rd. 2	M11	35
Park Grange Vw. 2	M12	35
Park Gro., Bram. 66	Y 5	19
Park Hill, Eck. 31	T18	59
Park House La. 9	Q 8	25
Park La. 10	J11	34
Park La., Thry. 65	W 3	8
Park Nook, Thry. 65	W 3	8
Park Rd. 6	G 9	21
Park Rd., Roth. 65	U 4	17
Park Spring Dr. 2	M12	35
Park Spring Gro. 2	M12	35
Park Spring Pl. 2	M12	35
Park Spring Way 2	M12	35
Park Sq. 1	L10	35
Park St., Raw. 62	T 1	7
Park St., Roth. 61	R 4	16
Park St., Swall. 31	U12	39
Park Vale Dr., Thry. 65	W 3	8
Park View Av. 19	T16	59
Park View Rd. 6	J 7	22
Park View Rd., Roth. 61	P 5	15
Park View Ter. 9	P 9	25
Greenland Rd.		
Park Vw., Roth. 61	Q 5	15
Parkers La. 10	J10	34
Parkers La. 17	F16	52
Parkers Rd. 10	J10	34
Parkfield Pl. 2	L12	35
St. Barnabas Rd.		
Parkfield Rd., Roth. 65	T 5	17
Parkgate Row, Raw. 62	T 3	7
Parkhead Cres. 11	G14	43
Parkhead Ct. 11	G14	43
Parkhead Rd. 11	G14	43
Parkside La., Stan. 6	F 9	20
Parkside Rd. 6	J 7	22
Parkson Rd., Roth. 60	U 7	27
Parkstone Delph 12	O15	46
Parkway Av. 9	N10	36
Parkway Clo. 9	N10	36
Parkway Dr. 9	O10	36
Parkwood Rd. 3	K 7	22
Parkwood Rd. N. 5	K 7	22
Parsley Hay Clo. 13	Q11	37
Parsley Hay Dr. 13	Q11	37
Parsley Hay Rd. 13	Q11	37
Parson Cross Rd. 6	J 6	12
Parsonage Clo. 19	S17	58
Parsonage Cres. 6	J 9	22
Parsonage St. 6	J 9	22
Partridge Vw. 2	N11	36
Skye Edge Av.		
Pass Houses Rd. 4	L 8	23
Paternoster Row 1	L11	35
Patmore Rd. 5	M 6	13
Paulet Rd. 2	O11	36
Pavement, The 2	L10	35
Duke St.		
Pavilion La., Brin. 60	R 7	26
Pawson Pl. 7	L12	35
Paxton Ct. 14	N14	46
Paxton La. 10	J11	34
Clarkehouse Rd.		
Payler Clo. 2	O12	36
Payne Cres., Raw. 62	T 1	7
Peacock Clo., Th.Hes. 61	N 1	4
Peakdale Cres. 12	Q13	47
Pear St. 11	K11	34
Pear Tree Av., Bram. 66	Y 5	19
Pear Tree Clo., Brin. 60	S 8	26
Pear Tree Rd. 5	M 5	13
Pearce Rd. 9	P10	37
Pearce Wk. 9	P10	37
Pearl St. 11	K12	34
Pearson Pl. 8	K14	44
Pearsons Clo., Roth. 65	V 6	18
Peashill La., Raw. 62	T 1	7
Peashill St., Raw. 62	T 1	7
Pedley Av., Mosb. 19	T15	49
Pedley Clo., Mosb. 19	T15	49
Pedley Dr., Mosb. 19	T16	59
Pedley Gro., Mosb. 19	T15	49
Peel St. 10	J11	34
Peel St., Roth. 60	S 4	16
Peel Ter. 10	K10	34
Wilkinson St.		
Peggy La. 30	N 4	14
Pembrey Ct., Btn. 19	U14	49
Pembroke St. 11	K11	34
Pembroke St., Roth. 61	Q 5	15
Pendeen Rd. 11	G12	33
Nethergreen Rd.		
Penistone Rd. 6	J 7	22
Penistone Rd. N. 6	J 6	12
Penistone Rd., Gren. 30	J 4	12
Penley St. 11	K12	34
Penns Rd. 2	M13	45
Penny La. 17	F17	52
Penrhyn Rd. 11	J12	34
Penrith Clo. 5	K 7	22
Penrith Cres. 5	K 7	22
Penrith Rd. 5	K 7	22
Penrose Pl. 13	R13	48
Penthorpe Clo. 12	O13	46
Pentland Gdns., Hack. 19	S15	48
Penton St. 1	L10	35
Pepper Clo., Roth. 61	P 2	5
Percy St. 3	K 9	22
Percy St., Roth. 65	T 5	17
Perigree Rd. 8	K14	44
Periwood La. 8	K14	44
Perkyn Rd. 5	M 4	13
Perkyn Ter. 5	M 4	13
Peter St., Roth. 61	Q 4	15
Peterborough Clo. 10	E11	32
Peterborough Dr. 10	E11	32
Peterborough Rd. 10	E11	32
Petre Dr. 4	N 8	24
Petre St. 4	M 9	23
Petworth Dr. 11	G15	43
Peveril Rd. 11	H12	33
Peveril Rd., Eck. 31	T18	59
Pexton Rd. 4	M 8	23
Philips Row, Raw. 62	T 1	7
Phillimore Rd. 9	O 9	24

102

Name	Grid	Page
Rosemary Rd., Wick. 66	X 5	19
Roslin Rd. 10	J10	34
Ross St. 9	P10	37
Rosser Av. 12	N15	46
Rossette Mt., Bram. 66	X 5	19
Rossington Rd. 11	J12	34
Rossiter Rd., Roth. 61	S 2	6
Rothay Rd. 4	N 7	24
Rothbury Clo. 19	U15	49
Rothbury Ct. 19	U15	49
Hartland Av.		
Rother Cres., Tree. 60	T10	39
Rother Rd., Roth. 60	S 6	16
Rother Ter., Roth. 60	S 6	16
Rother Vale Clo., Btn. 19	U14	49
Rother View Pl., Roth. 60	S 6	16
Rother View Rd., Roth. 60	S 6	16
Rotherham Rd. 13	R11	38
Rotherham Rd. N. 19	T16	59
Rotherham Rd., Th.Hes. 61	N 2	4
Rotherham Rd., Raw. 60 & 62	T 3	7
Rotherham Rd., Swall. 31	U12	39
Rotherham Rd., Btn. 19	U14	49
Rotherham Rd., Cat. 60	S 9	26
Rotherham Rd., Eck. 31	T18	59
Rotherham Rd., Mosb. 19	T17	59
Rotherham St. 9	O 8	24
Rotherhill Clo., Roth. 65	U 4	17
Rotherstoke Clo. 60	T 6	17
Rothervalley Way 19	U14	49
Rotherwood Av., Wd.M. 13	S12	38
Rotherwood Cres., Thur. 66	Y 9	29
Rough La., Gren. 30	H 4	11
Roughwood Grn., Roth. 61	R 2	6
Roughwood Rd., Roth. 61	Q 3	5
Roundel St. 9	N 9	24
Roundwood Gro., Raw. 62	U 1	7
Rowan Dr., Bram. 66	Y 5	19
Rowan Tree Dell 17	G18	53
Rowborn Dr., Ought. 30	G 6	11
Rowdale Cres. 12	P13	47
Rowel La., Lox. 6	E 8	20
Rowena Dr., Thur. 66	Y 8	29
Rowland Rd. 2	L12	35
Rowland St. 3	L 9	23
Harvest La.		
Rowsley St. 2	L11	35
Roxton Av. 8	K15	45
Roxton Rd. 8	K15	44
Roydfield Clo. 19	S15	48
Roydfield Dr. 19	S15	48
Roydfield Gro. 19	S15	48
Royds Av., Whis. 60	V 7	28
Royds Close Cres., Thry. 65	W 3	8
Royds Mill St. 4	M 9	23
Royds Moor Hill, Whis. 60	W 7	28
Royston Av. 19	R15	48
Royston Cft. 19	R15	48
Royston Clo. 19	R15	48
Royston Av.		
Royston Gro. 19	R15	48
Royston Av.		
Rudyard Rd. 6	J 8	22
Rufford Ct., Btn. 19	U15	49
Rufford Ri., Btn. 19	U15	49
Rugby St. 3	L 9	23
Rundle Dr. 7	K12	34
Rundle Rd. 7	K12	34
Rupert Rd. 7	K13	44
Rural La. 6	G 7	21
Rushby St. 4	M 7	23
Rushdale Av. 8	L13	45
Rushdale Mt. 8	L13	45
Rushdale Rd.		
Rushdale Rd. 8	L13	45
Rushdale Ter. 8	L13	45
Rushdale Rd.		
Rushley Av. 17	F16	52
Rushley Clo. 17	F16	52
Rushley Dr. 17	F16	52
Rushley Rd. 17	F16	52
Ruskin Sq. 8	L13	45
Russell Ct. 11	H14	43
Russell St. 3	L 9	23
Russell St., Roth. 65	T 4	17
Rustlings Rd. 11	H12	33
Rustlings Vw. 11	H12	33
Ruth Sq. 10	K11	34
Ruthin St. 4	N 8	24
Rutland Pk. 10	J11	34
Rutland Rd. 3	K 9	22
Rutland St. 3	K 9	22
Rutland Way 3	K 9	22
Rydal Rd. 8	K13	44
Rydalhurst Av. 6	G 7	21
Rye Bank, Whis. 60	V 7	28
Ryecroft Av. 17	F16	52
Ryecroft Glen Rd. 17	G16	53
Ryecroft Rd., Raw. 62	V 1	8
Ryecroft Vw. 17	F16	52
Ryefield Gdns. 11	H13	43
Ryegate Cres. 10	H10	33
Ryegate Rd. 10	H11	33
Ryeview Gdns., Roth. 61	R 3	6
Ryhill Dr., Hack. 19	R15	48
Ryle Rd. 7	K12	34
Rylstone Ct. 12	R14	48
Rylstone Gro.		
Rylstone Gro., Hack. 12	R14	48
Sackville Rd. 10	H10	33
Saddler Av. 19	S15	48
Saddler Clo. 19	S15	48
Saddler Grn. 19	S15	48
Saddler Gro. 19	S15	48
St. Aidans Av. 2	M12	35
St. Aidans Clo. 2	N11	36
St. Aidans Dr. 2	N11	36
St. Aidans Mt. 2	N12	36
St. Aidans Pl. 2	N12	36
St. Aidans Rd. 2	N11	36
St. Aidans Way 2	N12	36
St. Albans Clo. 10	E11	32
St. Albans Dr. 10	E11	32
St. Albans Rd. 10	E11	32
St. Albans Way, Wick. 66	X 6	19
St. Andrews Clo. 11	J12	34
St. Andrews Rd. 11	J12	34
St. Andrews Wk., Brin. 60	R 7	26
St. Anns Flats, Roth. 65	T 4	17
St. Anns Rd., Roth. 65	T 4	17
St. Anns, Roth. 65	T 4	17
St. Anthony Rd. 10	H10	33
St. Barnabas La. 2	L12	35
St. Barnabas Rd.		
St. Barnabas Rd. 2	L12	35
St. Charles St. 3	N 9	24
St. Davids Dr., Brin. 60	R 7	26
St. Elizabeth Clo. 2	L12	35
St. Georges Clo. 3	K10	34
St. Georges Dr., Brin. 60	R 7	26
St. Georges Sq. 1	K10	34
Portobello St.		
St. Georges Ter. 3	K10	34
St. James Dr., Rav. 65	Y 2	9
St. James Row 1	L10	35
St. James St. 1	L10	35
St. James Vw., Rav. 65	Y 2	9
St. Johns Av., Roth. 60	R 5	16
St. Johns Clo. 2	M10	35
St. Johns Rd. 2	M10	35
St. Johns Rd., Roth. 65	U 4	17
St. Johns Wk. 2	M10	35
St. Josephs Rd. 13	Q11	37
St. Lawrence Rd. 9	Q 6	15
St. Leonards Av., Thry. 65	W 3	8
St. Leonards La., Roth. 65	T 4	17
St. Leonards Rd., Roth. 65	T 4	17
St. Margarets Rd., Eccl. 30	L 4	13
St. Marks Cres. 10	J11	34
Glossop Rd.		
St. Marys Gate 2	K11	34
St. Marys La. 5	L 4	13
St. Marys Rd. 1 & 2	L11	35
St. Marys Rd., Raw. 62	U 1	7
St. Marys Sq. 2	K11	34
St. Marys Vw., Roth. 61	R 2	6
St. Michaels Clo., Eccl. 30	L 4	13
St. Michaels Cres., Eccl. 30	L 4	13
St. Michaels Rd., Eccl. 30	L 4	13
St. Nicholas Rd., Raw. 62	U 1	7
St. Pauls Par. 1	L10	35
Pinstone St.		
St. Peters Clo. 1	L10	35
Hartshead		
St. Philips La. 3	K 9	22
St. Philips Rd.		
St. Philips Rd. 3	K10	34
St. Quentin Clo. 17	H17	53
St. Quentin Dr. 17	H17	53
St. Quentin Mt. 17	H17	53
St. Quentin Ri. 17	H17	53
St. Quentin Vw. 17	H17	53
St. Ronans Rd. 7	K12	34
St. Stephens Rd., Roth. 65	T 4	17
St. Stephens Wk. 3	K10	34
St. Thomas Rd. 10	H10	33
St. Thomas St. 1	K10	34
St. Wilfrids Rd. 2	L12	35
St. Withold Av., Thur. 66	Y 9	29
St. Withold Av., Thur. 66	Y 9	29
Sale Hill 10	H11	33
Salisbury Rd. 10	H10	33
Salmon St. 11	K12	34
Salt Box La., Gren. 30	J 4	12
Samson St. 2	M10	35
Duke St.		
Samuel Clo. 2	M12	35
Samuel Dr. 2	M12	35
Samuel Pl. 2	M12	35
Samuel Rd. 2	M12	35
Sandbeck Pl. 11	J12	34
Sandbed Rd. 3	K 8	22
Sandberg Rd., Roth. 61	Q 3	5
Sandby Cft. 14	N15	46
Sandby Dr.		
Sandby Ct. 14	N15	46
Sandby Dr. 14	N15	46
Sandeby Dr., Rav. 65	Y 4	19
Sanderson Rd. 9	O 7	24
Sanderson St. 9	N 8	24
Sandford Grove Rd. 7	K13	44
Sandhill Clo., Raw. 62	U 1	7
Sandhurst Pl. 10	J10	34
Cobden View Rd.		
Sandpiper Rd., Th.Hes. 61	N 1	4
Sandringham Av., Whis. 60	U 7	27
Sandringham Pl., Rav. 65	Y 4	19
Sandringham Rd. 9	O 6	14
Newman Rd.		
Sands Clo. 14	N14	46
Sandstone Av. 4	N 7	24

Street	Ref.
Sandstone Clo. 5	O 6 14
Sandstone Dr. 4	N 7 24
Sandstone Rd. 4	N 7 24
Sandstone Vw. 4	N 7 24
Sandy Acres Clo. 19	T15 49
Sandy Acres Dr. 19	T15 49
Sandy Flat La., Wick. 66	X 7 29
Sandygate Gro. 10	F11 32
Sandygate La. 10	G11 33
Sandygate Park Cres. 10	F11 32
Sandygate Park Rd. 10	F10 32
Sandygate Pk. 10	F11 32
Sandygate Rd. 10	F11 32
Sarah St., Roth. 61	R 5 16
Sark Rd. 2	L12 35
London Rd.	
Saunders Pl. 2	N10 36
Saunders Rd. 2	N10 36
Savage La. 17	F16 52
Savile St. 4	M 9 23
Savile St. E. 4	M 9 23
Saville Rd., Whis. 60	U 7 27
Saville St., Dal.M. 65	V 3 8
Sawden Rd. 11	K11 34
Pomona St.	
Saxon Lea Av. 2	P11 37
Saxon Lea Cres. 2	P11 37
Saxon Lea Ct. 2	P11 37
Saxon Lea Dr. 2	P11 37
Saxon Rd. 8	L13 45
Saxton Dr., Roth. 60	T 7 27
Scammadine Clo., Brin. 60	S 8 26
Scarborough Rd. 9	P 9 25
Scarborough Rd., Wick. 66	X 5 19
Scargill Cft. 1	L10 35
Bank St.	
Scarlett Oak Meadow 6	F 9 20
Scarsdale Rd. 8	K14 44
Scholes La., Sch. 61	O 1 4
Scholes Vw., Eccl. 30	L 4 13
Scholey Rd., Wick. 66	X 5 19
Scholey St. 3	L 9 23
Wicker	
School Av. 19	T16 59
School Clo. 19	T16 59
School Green La. 10	E12 32
School Hill, Whis. 60	U 7 27
School La. 2	M10 35
Duke St.	
School La., Greenhill 8	K16 54
School La., Gren. 30	J 4 12
School La., Marsh. 31	Q18 57
School La., Norton 8	M15 45
School La., Raw. 62	T 2 7
School La., Stan. 6	F 9 20
School La., Thry. 65	W 2 8
School Lane Clo. 8	M15 45
School Rd. 10	H10 33
School Rd., Btn. 19	U14 49
School St. 2	M10 35
School St., Eck. 31	S18 58
School St., Mosb. 19	S16 58
School St., Roth. 65	U 4 17
School St., Swall. 31	U12 39
School St., Thry. 65	W 3 8
Scotia Clo. 2	N12 36
Scotia Dr. 2	N12 36
Scotland St. 3	K10 34
Scott Rd. 4	L 8 23
Scott St. 4	N 8 24
Scovell Av., Raw. 62	S 1 6
Scowerdons Clo. 12	Q13 47
Scowerdons Dr. 12	Q13 47
Scraith Wood Dr. 5	K 7 22
Scrooby Dr., Roth. 61	S 2 6
Scrooby La., Roth. 61	S 2 6
Scrooby St., Roth. 61	S 2 6
Seabreeze Ter. 13	P12 37
Richmond Rd.	
Seabrook Rd. 2	M11 35
Brierley Rd.	
Seagrave Av. 12	O14 46
Seagrave Cres. 12	O14 46
Seagrave Dr. 12	O14 46
Seagrave Rd. 12	O14 46
Searby Rd., Rav. 65	Y 4 19
Seaton Clo. 2	N11 36
Seaton Cres. 2	N10 36
Seaton Pl. 2	N11 36
Seaton Way 2	N11 36
Sebastian Vw., Brin. 60	S 7 26
Augustus Rd.	
Second La., Wick. 66	Y 7 29
Sedan St. 4	M 8 23
Seddons Clo., Roth. 61	Q 3 5
Sedgley Rd. 6	J 8 22
Sefton Rd. 10	F12 32
Selborne Rd. 10	H10 33
Selborne St. 9	N 9 24
Selborne St., Roth. 65	T 4 17
Selby Rd. 4	M 7 23
Sellars Rd., Roth. 61	Q 3 5
Sellers St. 8	K12 34
Selly Oak Gro. 8	M17 55
Selly Oak Rd. 8	M17 55
Selwyn St., Roth. 65	T 4 17
Senior Rd. 9	P10 37
Serpentine Wk. 8	L16 55
Sevenfields Ct. 6	H 7 21
Sevenfields La. 6	H 7 21
Severn Ct. 10	J10 34
Severn Rd. 10	J10 34
Severnside Dr. 13	R12 38
Severnside Gdns. 13	R12 38
Severnside Pl. 13	R12 38
Severnside Wk. 13	R13 48
Sewell Rd. 19	T17 59
Sexton Dr., Bram. 66	Y 6 19
Shafton Rd., Roth. 60	U 7 27
Shakespeare Rd., Roth. 65	T 4 17
Shalesmoor 3	K 9 22
Sharpe Av. 8	K16 54
Sharrard Clo. 12	O13 46
Sharrard Dr. 12	O13 46
Sharrard Gro. 12	O13 46
Sharrard Rd. 12	O13 46
Sharrow La. 11	K12 34
Sharrow Mount Cotts. 11	J12 34
Psalter La.	
Sharrow Mt. 11	J12 34
Psalter La.	
Sharrow St. 11	K12 34
Sharrow Vale Rd. 11	J12 34
Sharrow Vw. 7	K12 34
Shaw Rd., Roth. 65	U 4 17
Shaw St. 9	O 7 24
Shaw St., C.A. 18	M18 55
Shawsfield Rd., Roth. 61	T 6 17
Sheaf Av. 8	K13 44
Abbeydale Rd.	
Sheaf Bank 2	L12 35
Gleadless Rd.	
Sheaf Gardens Ter. 2	L11 35
Sheaf Gdns. 2	L11 35
Sheaf Sq. 1	L11 35
Sheaf St. 1 & 2	L10 35
Shearman Av., Roth. 61	Q 3 5
Shearwood Rd. 10	J10 34
Sheep Cote Rd., Roth. 60	V 6 18
Sheephill Rd. 11	E15 41
Sheffield La., Cat. 60	R 9 26
Sheffield Parkway 2 & 9	N10 36
Sheffield Parkway, Roth. 60	Q 9 25
Sheffield Rd., Dron. 18	K18 54
Sheffield Rd., Hack. 12	Q15 47
Sheffield Rd., Mosb. 19 & 31	S17 58
Sheffield Rd., Roth. 60	R 6 16
Sheffield Rd., Tinsley 9	P 7 25
Sheffield Rd., Wd.M. 13 & 31	T12 39
Sheffield Rd., Wood. 13	R13 48
Sheldon La., Stan. 6	F 9 20
Sheldon Rd. 7	K13 44
Sheldon Row 3	L10 35
Sheldon St. 2	K11 34
Shelley Clo., Roth. 65	U 5 17
Shelley Rd., Roth. 65	U 5 17
Shenstone Dr., Roth. 65	U 6 17
Shenstone Rd. 6	H 7 21
Shenstone Rd., Roth. 65	U 6 17
Shepcote La. 9	P 8 25
Shepcote Way 9	P 8 25
Shepherd St. 3	K10 34
Shepperson Rd. 6	H 7 21
Sherde Rd. 6	J 9 22
Sheridan Dr., Roth. 65	V 5 18
Sherrington Rd. 7	K12 34
Sherwood Cres., Roth. 60	T 5 17
Sherwood Glen 7	H15 43
Ship Hill, Roth. 60	S 5 16
Shipman Ct. 19	S16 58
School St.	
Shipton St. 6	K 9 22
Shirebrook Rd. 8	L13 45
Shirecliffe Clo. 3	L 8 23
Shirecliffe La. 3	L 8 23
Shirecliffe Rd. 5	L 7 23
Shiregreen La. 5	N 6 14
Shiregreen Ter. 5	M 5 13
Shirehall Cres. 5	M 4 13
Shirehall Rd. 5	M 5 13
Shirland La. 9	N 9 24
Shirley Rd. 3	L 8 23
Shore La. 10	H11 33
Shoreham Av., Roth. 60	T 7 27
Shoreham Dr., Roth. 60	T 7 27
Shoreham St. 1 & 2	L12 35
Short La. 6	D10 31
Shortbrook Bank, Mosb. 19	T16 59
Shortbrook Clo., Mosb. 19	T16 59
Shortbrook Croft, Mosb. 19	T16 59
Shortbrook Dr., Mosb. 19	T16 59
Shortbrook Rd., Mosb. 19	T16 59
Shortbrook Way, Mosb. 19	T16 59
Shortbrook Wk. 19	T16 59
Shortridge St. 9	N 9 24
Shorts La. 17	E17 52
Whitelow La.	
Shrewsbury Rd. 2	L11 35
Shrewsbury Ter., Roth. 61	Q 5 15
Shrogs Wood Rd., Roth. 60	V 6 18
Shubert Clo. 13	R12 38
Shude Hill 1	L10 35
Shude La. 1	L10 35
Sicey Av. 5	M 4 13
Sicey La. 5	M 5 13
Sicklebrook La., C.A. 18	N18 56
Siddall St. 1	K10 34
Sidney St. 1	L11 35
Siemens Clo. 9	Q 7 25
Silkstone Clo. 12	Q14 47
Silkstone Cres. 12	Q14 47
Silkstone Dr. 12	P14 47
Silkstone Pl. 12	Q14 47
Silkstone Rd. 12	Q14 47
Silver Birch Av. 10	F12 32
Silver Hill Rd. 11	H13 43
Silver Mill Rd. 2	L12 35
Silver St. 1	L10 35
Silver St., Thry. 65	W 3 8
Silver Street Head 1	L10 35
Silverdale Clo. 11	H13 43

Silverdale Cres. 11	H13	43
Silverdale Croft 11	H13	43
Silverdale Gdns. 11	H13	43
Silverdale Glade 11	H13	43
Silverdale Rd. 11	H14	43
Silvermoor Dr., Rav. 65	Y 4	19
Simmonite Rd., Roth. 61	Q 3	5
Singleton Gro. 6	J 8	22
Singleton Rd. 6	J 8	22
Sitwell Dr., Roth. 60	T 6	17
Sitwell Gro., Roth. 60	U 7	27
Sitwell La., Wick. 66	X 6	19
Sitwell Park Rd., Roth. 60	V 6	18
Sitwell Pl. 7	K12	34
London Rd.		
Sitwell Rd. 7	K12	34
Sitwell St., Eck. 31	S18	58
Sitwell Vale, Roth. 60	T 6	17
Skelton Clo. 13	R13	48
Skelton Dr. 13	R13	48
Skelton Gro. 13	R13	48
Skelton La., Btn. 19	T14	49
Skelton La., Wood. 13	R13	48
Skelton Rd. 8	L13	45
Skelton Ri., Ought. 30	F 5	10
Skelton Way 13	R13	48
Skelton Wk. 13	S13	48
Skelwith Clo. 4	N 7	24
Skelwith Dr. 4	N 7	24
Skew Hill La., Gren. 30	H 4	11
Skew Hill, Gren. 30	J 4	12
Skinnerthorpe Rd. 4	M 7	23
Skipton Rd. 4	M 8	23
Skye Edge Av. 2	M11	35
Skye Edge Rd. 2	M11	35
Slacks La., Bram. 66	Y 6	19
Slate St. 2	L12	35
Slayleigh Av. 10	F12	32
Slayleigh Dr. 10	F12	32
Slayleigh La. 10	F12	32
Sleaford St. 9	N 9	24
Sledgate Clo., Wick. 66	W 6	18
Sledgate La., Wick. 66	W 6	18
Slinn St. 10	J 9	22
Slitting Mill La. 9	N 9	24
Oakes Grn.		
Sload La., Ridg. 12	P17	57
Smallage La., Wd.M. 13	U11	39
Smalldale Rd. 12	P14	47
Smeaton St. 11	K12	34
Smelter Wood Av. 13	Q12	37
Smelter Wood Clo. 13	Q12	37
Smelter Wood Cres. 13	Q12	37
Smelter Wood Dr. 13	Q12	37
Smelter Wood La. 13	Q12	37
Smelter Wood Pl. 13	Q12	37
Smelter Wood Rd. 13	Q12	37
Smelter Wood Ri. 13	Q12	37
Smelter Wood Way 13	Q12	37
Smith St. 9	P 9	25
Smithfield 3	L10	35
Smithfield Rd. 12	O15	46
Smithy Clo., Roth. 61	Q 3	5
Smithy Croft, D.Wd. 18	J18	54
Smithy Wood Cres. 8	K14	44
Smithy Wood Rd. 8	K14	44
Snail Hill, Roth. 60	S 5	16
Snaithing La. 10	G11	33
Snaithing Park Clo. 10	G11	33
Snaithing Park Rd. 10	G11	33
Snape Hill Clo., Dron. 18	L18	55
Snape Hill Cres., Dron. 18	L18	55
Snape Hill La., Dron. 18	L18	55
Snig Hill 3	L10	35
Snow Hill 2	M10	35
Snow La. 3	L10	35
Snowdon La., Marsh. 31	O18	56
Snowdon Way, Brin. 60	S 8	26
Soap House La. 13	T12	39
Solly St. 1	K10	34
Somercotes Rd. 12	P13	47
Somerset Rd. 3	L 9	23
Somerset St. 3	L 9	23
Somerville Ter. 6	J 9	22
Sopewell Rd., Roth. 61	P 5	15
Sorby St. 4	M 9	23
Sorby Way, Wick. 66	X 6	19
Sorrel Rd., Bram. 66	Y 5	19
Sorrell Hill 6	J 6	12
Fox Hill Rd.		
Sorrelsykes Clo., Whis. 60	U 8	27
Sothall Clo. 19	T14	49
Sothall Ct., Btn. 19	T14	49
Sothall Grn. 19	T14	49
Sough Hall Av., Th.Hes. 61	N 1	4
Sough Hall Clo., Th.Hes. 61	N 1	4
Sough Hall Cres., Th.Hes. 61	N 1	4
Sough Hall Rd., Th.Hes. 61	N 2	4
Soughley La. 10	C12	31
South Cres., Roth. 65	U 4	17
South La. 1	L11	35
South Par. 3	L 9	23
South Rd. 6	J 9	22
South Rd., Roth. 61	Q 4	15
South St. 2	M10	35
South St., Greas. 61	S 2	6
South St., Mosb. 19	S17	58
South St., Raw. 62	U 1	7
South St., Roth. 61	Q 5	15
South Vale Dr., Thry. 65	W 3	8
South View Clo. 6	G 7	21
South View Cres. 7	K12	34
South View Rd. 7	K12	34
South View Ri., Lox. 6	G 7	21
South View Ter., Cat. 60	S 9	26
South Vw. 19	U16	59
Southall St. 8	L13	45
Arthington St.		
Southbourne Rd. 10	J11	34
Southcroft Gdns. 7	K12	34
Southcroft Wk. 7	K12	34
Southend Pl. 2	N11	36
Southend Rd. 2	N11	36
Southey Av. 5	L 6	13
Southey Clo. 5	K 6	12
Southey Cres. 5	K 6	12
Southey Dr. 5	L 6	13
Southey Green Clo. 5	K 6	12
Southey Green Rd. 5	K 6	12
Southey Hall Dr. 5	K 6	12
Southey Hall Rd. 5	K 6	12
Southey Hill 5	K 6	12
Southey Pl. 5	K 6	12
Southey Ri. 5	K 6	12
Southey Wk. 5	K 6	12
Southgate, Eck. 31	T18	59
Southgrove Rd. 10	J11	34
Southsea Rd. 13	R13	48
Southwell Rd. 4	N 7	24
Spa Brook Clo. 12	Q13	47
Spa Brook Dr. 12	Q13	47
Spa La. 13	S13	48
Spa Lane Cft., Wood. 13	S13	48
Spa View Av. 12	Q14	47
Spa View Dr. 12	Q14	47
Spa View Pl. 12	Q14	47
Spa View Rd. 12	Q14	47
Spa View Ter. 12	Q14	47
Spa View Way 12	Q14	47
Spa Well Cres., Tree. 60	T 9	27
Spalton Rd., Raw. 62	T 2	7
Speeton Rd. 6	J 8	22
Spencer Dr., Rav. 65	Y 4	19
Spencer Rd. 2	L12	35
Spenser Rd., Roth. 65	U 5	17
Spinkhill Av. 13	P12	37
Spinkhill Dr. 13	P12	37
Spinkhill Rd. 13	P12	37
Spinney Clo., Roth. 60	U 6	17
Spinneyfield, Roth. 60	U 7	27
Spital Hill 4	L 9	23
Spital La. 3	M 9	23
Spital St. 3	L 9	23
Spitalfields 3	L 9	23
Spofforth Rd. 9	O 9	24
Harry Firth Clo.		
Spoon Glade 6	E 8	20
Spoon La., Stan. 6	E 9	20
Spoon Ms. 6	F 9	10
Spoon Way 6	F 9	20
Spooner Rd. 10	J10	34
Spoonhill Rd. 6	G 9	21
Acorn Dr.		
Spotswood Clo. 14	N14	46
Spotswood Dr. 14	N13	46
Spotswood Mt. 14	M14	46
Spotswood Pl. 14	M14	45
Spotswood Rd. 14	M14	45
Spout Copse 6	F 9	10
Acorn Dr.		
Spout La., Stan. 6	E 9	20
Spout Spinney, Stan. 6	E 9	20
Spring Clo. 7	J14	44
Spring Close Dell 14	N14	46
Spring Close Mt. 14	N14	46
Spring Close Vw. 14	N14	46
Spring Croft, Roth. 61	Q 3	5
Spring Garden La., Wick. 66	X 6	19
Spring Hill 10	J10	34
Spring Hill Rd. 10	J10	34
Spring House Rd. 10	J10	34
Spring La. 2	N12	36
Spring St. 3	L10	35
Spring St., Roth. 65	T 4	17
Spring Vale Rd. 6 & 10	H10	33
Spring View Rd. 10	J10	34
Spring Water Av. 12	R14	48
Spring Water Clo. 12	R14	48
Spring Water Dr. 12	R14	48
Springfield Av. 7	J13	44
Springfield Clo. 7	J14	44
Springfield Dr., Thry. 65	X 3	9
Springfield Glen 7	H14	43
Springfield Rd. 7	J14	44
Springfield Rd., Wick. 66	X 5	19
Springvale Clo., Wick. 66	Y 7	29
Springvale Wk. 6	J 9	22
Springwood Rd. 8	L13	45
Spruce Av., Wick. 66	X 5	19
Spurr St. 2	L12	35
Square, E., The, Bram. 66	Y 4	19
Square, W., The, Bram. 66	X 4	19
Squirrel Gro. 61	Q 2	5
Stacye Av. 13	S13	48
Stacye Ri. 13	S13	48
Stadium Ct. 61	S 3	6
Stafford Cres., Roth. 60	T 7	27
Stafford Dr., Roth. 60	T 7	27
Stafford La. 2	M11	35
Stafford Ms. 2	M11	35
Stafford La.		
Stafford Pl., Th.Hes. 61	N 1	4
Stafford Rd. 2	M11	35
Stafford St. 2	M10	35
Stag Clo., Roth. 60	V 6	18
Stag Cres., Roth. 60	V 6	18
Stag La., Roth. 60	U 6	17
Stainmore Av., Btn. 19	U16	59
Stainton Rd. 11	H12	33
Stair Rd. 4	M 8	23
Stalker Lees Rd. 11	J12	34
Stalker Pl. 11	K11	34
Stalker Lees Rd.		

106

Street	Ref	Pg
Twickenham Glade, Mosb. 19	T17	59
Twickenham Glen, Mosb. 19	T17	59
Twickenham Gro., Mosb. 19	T17	59
Twigg St., Roth. 61	R4	16
Twitchill Dr. 13	R13	48
Tyas Rd. 5	L4	13
Tye Rd. 19	U14	49
Tyler St. 9	O7	24
Tyler Way 9	O6	14
Tylney Rd. 2	M11	35
Tynker Av., Btn. 19	U14	49
Tyzack Rd. 8	K15	44
Ulley Cres. 13	O12	36
Ulley Rd. 13	O12	36
Ullswater Av. 19	T17	59
Ullswater Clo. 19	T17	59
Ulrica Dr., Thur. 66	Y9	29
Ulverston Rd. 8	K14	44
Undercliffe Rd. 6	G9	21
Underhill La. 6	H5	11
Underwood Rd. 8	K14	44
Union La. 1	L11	35
Union La., Roth. 60	S5	16
Union Rd. 11	J13	44
Union St. 1	L11	35
Union St., Roth. 61	R5	16
Unstone St. 2	L11	35
John St.		
Uplands, Raw. 62	T1	7
Upper Albert Rd. 8	L13	45
Upper Allen St. 3	K10	34
Upper Clara St., Roth. 61	Q5	15
Upper Gate Rd., Stan. 61	E9	20
Upper Hanover St. 3	K10	34
Upper Millgate, Roth. 60	S5	16
Upper Rye Clo., Whis. 60	V7	28
Upper Valley Rd. 8	L13	45
Upper Whiston La., Whis. 60	V8	28
Upper Wortley Rd., Th.Hes. 61	N2	4
Upper Wortley Rd., Roth. 61	P4	15
Upperthorpe 6	J9	22
Upperthorpe Glen 6	J9	22
Upperthorpe Rd. 6	K9	22
Upwell Hill 4	N7	24
Upwell La. 4	N7	24
Upwell St. 4	N7	24
Upwood Rd. 6	H7	21
Uttley Clo. 9	O9	24
Uttley Croft 9	O9	24
Uttley Dr. 9	O9	24
Vainor Rd. 6	H7	21
Vale Av., Thry. 65	W3	8
Vale Gro. 6	G8	21
Vale Rd. 3	K8	22
Vale Rd., Thry. 65	W3	8
Valentine Clo. 5	M5	13
Valentine Cres. 5	M5	13
Valentine Rd. 5	M5	13
Valley Rd. 12	S14	48
Valley Rd. 8	L13	45
Varley Gdns., Bram. 66	X5	19
Redgrave Pl.		
Vauxhall Clo. 9	O6	14
Vauxhall Rd. 9	O6	14
Ventnor Pl. 7	K12	34
Venus Ct., Brin. 60	S7	26
Verdant Way 5	M5	13
Verdon St. 3	L9	23
Vere Rd. 6	J7	22
Vernon Delph 10	G10	33
Vernon Rd., Roth. 60	U6	17
Vernon Rd., Tot. 17	G17	53
Vernon Ter. 10	H11	33
Vesey St., Raw. 62	T2	7
Vestry St. 6	J10	34
Horam Rd.		
Vicar La. 1	L10	35
Vicar La., Wood. 13	R12	38
Vicarage Clo., Roth. 65	V4	18
Vicarage Cres., Gren. 30	J4	12
Vicarage La. 17	F16	52
Vicarage Rd. 9	N8	24
Vicarage Rd., Gren. 30	J4	12
Vickers Dr. 5	M6	13
Vickers Rd. 5	M7	23
Victor Rd. 17	G16	53
Victor St. 6	J8	22
Victoria Av., Roth. 65	T5	17
Victoria La., Roth. 60	S5	16
Victoria Rd. 10	K11	34
Victoria Rd., Btn. 19	T14	49
Victoria Rd., Raw. 62	T2	7
Victoria St. 3	K10	34
Victoria St., Cat. 60	S9	26
Victoria St., Roth. 60	R5	16
Victoria Station Rd. 4	L10	35
View Bank 8	L13	45
Artisan Vw.		
View Rd. 2	L12	35
View Rd., Roth. 65	U4	17
Village St., Wick. 66	X6	19
Villiers Clo. 2	N13	46
Villiers Dr. 2	N13	46
Vincent Rd. 7	K12	34
Vincent Rd., Rav. 65	Y4	19
Violet Av. 19	T14	49
Violet Bank Rd. 7	K13	44
Vivian Rd. 5	M7	23
Vulcan Rd. 9	O7	24
Wadbrough Rd. 11	J11	34
Waddell Dr., Brin. 60	S8	26
Wade Clo., Roth. 60	T6	17
Wade Meadow 6	H7	21
Wade St. 4	N7	24
Wadsley La. 6	H7	21
Wadsley Park Cres. 6	H7	21
Wadsworth Av. 12	P13	47
Wadsworth Clo. 12	P13	47
Wadsworth Dr.		
Wadsworth Dr. 12	P13	47
Wadsworth Rd. 12	P13	47
Wadsworth Av.		
Wadsworth Rd., Bram. 66	Y6	19
Wadsworth Ri., Dal.M. 65	W3	8
Brierley Rd.		
Wag La. 10	C13	41
Wagon Rd., Roth. 61	R2	6
Waingate 3	L10	35
Wainwright Av. 13	P12	37
Wainwright Cres. 13	P12	37
Wainwright Rd., Roth. 61	Q3	5
Wake Rd. 7	K12	34
Walden Rd. 2	L12	35
Walders Av. 6	H7	21
Wales Pl. 6	J9	22
Walk, The, Roth. 65	U4	17
Walker Clo., Gren. 30	H4	11
Walker St. 3	L9	23
Walker St., Roth. 61	U1	7
Walker Vw., Roth. 61	U1	7
Walkley Bank Clo. 6	J8	22
Walkley Bank Rd. 6	H9	21
Walkley Crescent Rd. 6	H9	21
Walkley La. 6	J8	22
Walkley Rd. 6	J9	22
Walkley St. 6	J9	22
Walkley Ter. 6	H9	21
Wallace Rd. 3	K8	22
Waller Rd. 6	H9	21
Walling Clo. 9	O7	24
Walling Rd. 9	O7	24
Walshaw Rd., Wor. 30	F5	10
Walter St. 6	J8	22
Burton St.		
Walter St., Roth. 60	S4	16
Waltham Gdns. 19	U15	49
Waltheof Rd. 2	O12	36
Walton Rd. 11	J11	34
Wannop St. 62	T2	7
Wansfell Rd. 4	N7	24
Wapping Back La.	Y1	9
Hoot.R. 65		
Warburton Clo. 2	M12	35
Warburton Gdns. 2	M12	35
Warburton Rd. 2	M12	35
Ward Pl. 7	K12	34
Ward St. 3	L9	23
Ward St., Roth. 61	R4	16
Warde Aldam Cres., Wick. 66	X5	19
Warden St., Roth. 60	S6	16
Wardlow Rd. 12	P13	47
Wardsend Rd. 5	J7	22
Wardsend Rd. N. 6	J6	12
Wareham Ct. 19	U15	49
Warley Rd. 2	N11	36
Warminster Clo. 8	L14	45
Warminster Cres. 8	L14	45
Warminster Dr. 8	L14	45
Warminster Gdns. 8	L15	45
Warminster Rd.		
Warminster Pl. 8	L15	45
Warminster Rd. 8	L14	45
Warner Rd. 6	H7	21
Warren Av., Raw. 62	T1	7
Warren Dr., Roth. 61	Q4	15
Warren Mt., Roth. 61	Q4	15
Warren Rd., Wick. 66	X5	19
Warren Ri., Dron. 18	M18	55
Warren St. 4	M9	23
Warren Vale Rd., Raw. 62	U1	7
Warrener Dr., Rav. 65	X3	9
Warrington Rd. 10	J10	34
Warris Clo., Roth. 61	Q3	5
Warris Pl. 2	M10	35
Warwick St. 10	J10	34
Warwick St. S., Roth. 60	T5	17
Warwick St., Roth. 60	T5	17
Warwick Ter. 10	J10	34
Warwick St.		
Wasdale Av. 19	T17	59
Wasdale Clo. 19	T17	59
Washfield Cres., Tree. 60	T10	39
Washfield La., Tree. 60	T10	39
Washford Rd. 9	N9	24
Washington Rd. 11	K11	34
Watch St. 13	T12	39
Water La. 3	M7	23
Snig Hill		
Water La., Dore 17	G16	53
Water La., Rav. 60	Y1	9
Water La., Roth. 60	S5	16
Water Slacks Clo. 13	R13	48
Water Slacks Dr. 13	R13	48
Water Slacks Rd. 13	R13	48
Water Slacks Way 13	R13	48
Water Slacks Wk. 13	R13	48
Water St. 3	L10	35
Waterfall Rd. 9	P9	25
Greenland Rd.		
Waterford Rd. 3	K8	22
Waterloo Wk. 6	K9	22
Cornish St.		
Watersmeet Rd. 6	H8	21
Waterthorpe Clo. 19	T16	59
Waterthorpe Cres. 19	T16	59
Waterthorpe Gdns. 19	T16	59
Waterthorpe Glade 19	T16	59
Waterthorpe Glen 19	T16	59
Waterthorpe Greenway 19	S14	48
Waterthorpe Ri. 19	T15	49
Watery St. 3	K9	22
Wath Rd. 7	K13	44
Watkin La. 6	K9	22
Infirmary Rd.		
Watkinson Gdns. 19	T15	49

Watson Glen, Roth. 61	P 4	15
Watson Rd. 10	J11	34
Watson Rd., Roth. 61	Q 4	15
Watsons Wk. 1	L10	35
Hartshead		
Watt La. 10	G11	33
Waverley Rd. 9	P10	37
Waverley Vw., Cat. 60	S 9	26
Wayland Rd. 11	J12	34
Weakland Clo. 12	Q15	47
Weakland Cres. 12	Q14	47
Weakland Dr. 12	Q14	47
Weakland Way 12	Q14	47
Webbs Av., Stan. 6	F 9	20
Webster Clo., Roth. 61	P 4	15
Webster Cres., Roth. 61	P 4	15
Webster St. 9	O 7	24
Weedon St. 9	O 7	24
Weetwood Dr. 11	H13	43
Weetwood Rd., Roth. 60	U 7	27
Weir Head 9	O 7	24
Welbeck Ri., Roth. 65	U 4	17
Welbeck Rd. 6	H 9	21
Welbury Gdns. 19	T17	59
Welby Pl. 8	K14	44
Welham Dr., Roth. 60	T 6	17
Well Ct. 12	R14	48
Well Green Rd., Stan. 6	E 9	20
Well La. 6	G 7	21
Well La., Tree. 60	T10	39
Well Meadow Dr. 3	K10	34
Well Meadow St. 3	K10	34
Well Pl. 8	L13	45
Well Rd.		
Well Rd. 8	L13	45
Well View Rd., Roth. 61	P 4	15
Welland Clo. 3	K 9	22
Wellcarr Rd. 8	L15	45
Wellesley Rd. 10	J10	34
Wellfield Clo.,	Q15	47
Ridg. 12		
Wellfield Rd. 6	J 9	22
Wellfield Rd., Roth. 61	Q 3	5
Wellgate Mt., Roth. 60	T 5	17
Wellgate, Roth. 60	S 5	16
Wellhead Rd. 8	L13	45
Welling Way, Roth. 61	Q 4	15
Wellington Pl. 9	P10	37
Main Rd.		
Wellington Rd. 6	G 9	21
Wellington St. 1	K11	34
Wells La., Whis. 60	V 8	28
Wellway, The, Bram. 66	X 4	19
Welney Pl. 6	J 6	12
Welwyn Clo. 2	O14	46
Welwyn Rd. 12	O14	46
Wenlock St. 13	Q11	37
Wensley Clo. 4	N 7	24
Wensley Croft 4	N 7	24
Wensley Dr. 4	N 7	24
Wensley Gdns. 4	N 7	24
Wensley Grn. 4	N 7	24
Wensley St. 4	N 7	24
Wensleydale Cres.,	Q 2	5
Roth. 61		
Wensleydale Dr.,	S 8	26
Brin. 60		
Wensleydale Rd.,	Q 2	5
Roth. 61		
Wentworth Av. 11	H14	43
Wentworth Clo.,	N 1	4
Th.Hes. 61		
Wentworth Pl. 61	P 3	5
Wentworth Rd.,	O 1	4
Th.Hes.61		
Wesley La. 10	H10	33
Wessex Gdns. 17	F17	52
West Av., Raw. 62	T 1	7
West Bank Clo., C.A. 18	L18	55
West Bank La. 1	L10	35
Trippet La.		
West Bar 3	L10	35
West Bawtry Rd.,	S 7	26
Roth. 60		
West Clo. 61	Q 4	15
West Don St. 6	K 9	22
West Hill La. 3	K10	34
West Hill, Roth. 61	P 5	15
West La., Aug. 31	U11	39
West La., Lox. 6	E 7	20
West Park Dr.,	U12	39
Swall. 31		
West Quadrant 5	M 6	13
West St. 1	K10	34
West St., Btn. 19	U14	49
West St., Eck. 31	S18	58
West St., Roth. 60	S 5	16
West Street La. 1	L10	35
Holly St.		
West Vale Gro., Thry. 65	W 3	8
West View Clo. 17	G17	53
West View La. 17	G17	53
West View Rd., Roth. 61	P 5	15
West Well Pl. 19	S17	58
Westbar Grn. 3	L10	35
Westbourne Rd. 10	J11	34
Westbrook Bank 11	J12	34
Westbury St. 9	N 9	24
Westby Cres., Whis. 60	U 7	27
Westcroft Cres.,	T16	59
Mosb. 19		
Westcroft Dr., Mosb. 19	T16	59
Westcroft Gdns.,	T16	59
Mosb. 19		
Westcroft Glen,	T16	59
Mosb. 19		
Westcroft Gro.,	T16	59
Mosb. 19		
Western Bank 10	J10	34
Western Rd. 10	H10	33
Western Rd., Roth. 65	U 4	17
Westfield Av. 12	S14	48
Westfield Centre,	T16	59
Mosb. 19		
Westfield Cres. 19	S16	58
Westfield Gro. 12	S14	48
Westfield Northway,	T15	49
Mosb. 19		
Westfield Rd., Bram. 66	Y 5	19
Westfield Rd., Raw. 62	T 2	7
Westfield Southway,	T16	59
Mosb. 19		
Westfield Ter. 1	K10	34
Westfield Vw., Roth. 60	S 5	16
Westgate, Roth. 60	S 5	16
Westland Clo., Mosb. 19	T15	49
Westland Gdns.,	S15	48
Mosb. 19		
Westland Gro.,	T16	59
Mosb. 19		
Westland Rd., Mosb. 19	S16	58
Westminster Av. 10	E11	32
Westminster Clo. 10	E11	32
Westminster Cres. 10	E11	32
Westmoreland St. 6	K 9	22
Westnall Rd. 5	M 4	13
Westnall Ter. 5	M 4	13
Weston St. 3	K10	34
Westover Rd. 10	G11	33
Westwick Cres. 8	K16	54
Westwick Gro. 8	K16	54
Westwick Rd. 8	J17	54
Westwood Rd. 11	G12	33
Wetherby Ct. 9	P10	37
Staniforth Rd.		
Wharf La. 9	P 6	15
Wharf St. 1	L10	35
Wharncliffe Rd. 10	K11	34
Wharncliffe St.,	T 4	17
Roth. 65		
Wheata Dr. 5	L 4	13
Wheata Pl. 5	L 4	13
Wheata Rd. 5	L 5	13
Wheatcroft Rd., Raw. 62	U 1	7
Wheatfield Cres. 5	M 5	13
Wheathill St., Roth. 60	S 5	16
Wheatley Gro. 13	Q11	37
Wheatley Rd., Roth. 61	Q 3	5
Wheats La. 1	L10	35
Paradise St.		
Wheel Hill 1	L10	35
Wheel La., Gren. 30	J 4	12
Wheel La., Ought. 30	F 4	10
Wheel, The 30	K 4	12
Wheldrake Rd. 5	M 7	23
Whinacre Clo. 8	L17	55
Whinacre Pl. 8	L17	55
Whinacre Wk. 8	L17	55
Whinfell Ct. 11	G15	43
Whinmoor Rd. 5	N 6	14
Whins, The,	S 1	6
Nether Haugh 62		
Whirlow Court Rd. 11	G15	43
Whirlow Farm Ms. 11	G14	43
Whirlow Gro. 11	G15	43
Whirlow La. 11	G14	43
Whirlow Park Rd. 11	G15	43
Whirlowdale Clo. 11	G15	43
Whirlowdale Cres. 7	H14	43
Whirlowdale Rd. 7 & 11	G15	43
Whirlowdale Ri. 11	G15	43
Whiston Brook Vw.,	V 7	28
Whis. 60		
Whiston Grange 60	U 7	27
Whiston Gro., Roth. 60	T 6	17
Whitby Rd. 9	P 9	25
White Cft. 1	L10	35
White Hill La., Brin. 60	S 7	26
White La. 12	O14	46
Whitecroft Cres.,	S 8	26
Brin. 60		
Whitegate Wk., Roth. 61	Q 2	5
Whitehall Rd., Roth. 61	Q 2	5
Whitehill Av., Brin. 60	S 8	26
Whitehill Dr., Brin. 60	S 8	26
Whitehill Rd., Brin. 60	R 8	26
Whitehorns Dr. 8	L17	55
Whitehouse La. 6	J 9	22
Whitehouse Rd. 6	J 9	22
Whiteley La. 10	F12	32
Whiteley Wood Clo. 11	G12	33
Whiteley Wood Rd.		
Whiteley Wood Rd. 11	G13	43
Whitelow La. 17	E16	52
Whites La. 2	M10	35
Whitethorns Clo. 8	L17	55
Whitethorns Dr. 8	L17	55
Whitethorns Vw. 8	L17	55
Whiteways Clo. 4	M 8	23
Whiteways Dr. 4	M 8	23
Whiteways Gro. 4	M 8	23
Whiteways Rd. 4	M 8	23
Whitfield Rd. 10	F12	32
Whitham Rd. 10	J11	34
Whiting St. 8	L13	45
Arthington St.		
Whitley View Rd.,	O 5	14
Roth. 61		
Whitwell St. 9	P10	37
Whitworth La. 9	O 8	24
Whitworth Rd. 10	G11	33
Whixley Rd. 9	O 9	24
Whybourne Gro.,	T 5	17
Roth. 60		
Whybourne Ter.,	T 5	17
Roth. 60		
Wicker 3	L10	35
Wicker La. 3	L10	35
Wickersley Rd.,	U 6	17
Roth. 60		
Wickfield Clo. 12	Q13	47
Wickfield Dr. 12	Q14	47
Wickfield Gro. 12	Q14	47
Wickfield Pl. 12	Q13	47
Wickfield Rd. 12	Q13	47
Widdop Cft. 13	P12	37
Widdop Clo. 13	P12	37
Wigfull Rd. 11	J11	34
Wignall Av., Wick. 66	W 6	18
Wilcox Clo. 6	J15	44
Wilcox Grn., Roth. 61	R 2	6
Wilcox Rd. 6	J 5	12

NOTES

BARNSLEY

Abbreviations

Cud., Cudworth; Dod., Dodsworth; Gaw., Gawber; Map., Mapplewell; Wor, Worsborough.

Street	Ref
Abbey La.	H 6 67
Abbey Sq.	G 4 62
Abbots Rd.	H 5 67
Acre Rd., Cud.	K 4 63
Agnes Rd.	D 7 65
Agnes Ter.	D 7 65
Day St.	
Ainsdale Ct.	G 3 62
Aireton Rd.	D 6 65
Prospect St.	
Albert St.	D 6 65
Albert St. E.	D 6 65
Albion Rd.	G 2 62
Albion Ter.	E 7 65
Aldbury Clo.	F 3 61
Alderson Dr.	E 3 61
Alexander Ter.	H 7 67
Allatt Clo.	D 7 65
Allendale Rd.	D 4 60
Alma St.	C 6 64
Almond Av., Cud.	J 2 63
Alperton Clo.	H 4 62
Ambleside Gro.	J 7 67
April Clo.	G 4 62
April Dr.	G 4 62
Aqueduct St.	D 4 60
Arcade, The	D 6 65
Ardsley Ms.	J 7 67
Arncliffe Dr.	B 6 64
Arnold Av.	D 2 60
Arundell Dr.	H 4 62
Ash Gro.	G 7 66
Ash Row	F 6 66
Ashbourne Rd.	E 2 61
Ashfield Clo.	C 5 64
Aston Dr.	E 3 61
Athersley Cres.	E 3 61
Athersley Rd.	F 3 61
Austwick Wk.	D 6 65
Prospect St.	
Avon St.	E 6 65
Aylesford Clo	D 5 65
Honeywell Pl.	
Aysgarth Av.	J 6 67
Back La.	F 4 61
Bailey St.	D 6 65
Baker St.	
Bainton Dr.	C 7 64
Baker St.	D 6 65
Bakewell Rd.	E 3 61
Balehouse La., Gaw.	B 5 64
Balk St.	E 6 65
Banford Av.	E 3 61
Bank St.	E 7 65
Bank St., Cud.	J 3 62
Bank St., Stairfoot	H 7 67
Bar La., Map.	C 2 60
Barnabas Wk.	D 5 65
Barnsley Rd.	F 5 66
Barnsley Rd., Cud.	J 3 63
Baslow Rd.	F 2 61
Batty Av., Cud.	J 3 63
Baycliff Clo.	G 3 62
Beachcroft Way	H 7 67
Beaconsfield St.	D 6 65
Beaumont Av.	B 6 64
Beckett Hospital Ter.	E 7 65
Dobie St.	
Beckett St.	E 5 65
Bedford St.	D 7 65
Bedford Ter.	E 4 61
Beech Av., Cud.	J 2 63
Beech Gro.	C 7 64
Beech St.	E 7 65
Beever La., Gaw.	B 5 64
Beevor St.	F 6 66
Belgrave Rd.	E 6 65
Belle Green La., Cud.	K 2 63
Belmont Av.	F 3 61
Belmont, Cud.	K 4 63
Bentham Dr.	G 4 62
Bentley Clo.	G 3 62
Berneslai Clo.	D 5 65
Bingley St.	C 5 64
Birch Rd.	G 7 66
Birchfield Wk.	B 5 64
Birk Av.	F 7 66
Birk Cres.	F 7 66
Birk Grn.	G 7 66
Birk House La.	G 7 66
Birk Rd.	F 7 66
Birk Ter.	F 7 66
Birkwood Av., Cud.	K 4 63
Bishops Way	F 5 66
Bismarck St.	D 7 65
Blackburn La.	C 5 64
Blackheath Clo.	F 2 61
Blackheath Rd.	F 3 61
Blackheath Wk.	F 2 61
Blakeley Clo.	F 2 61
Bleasdale Gro.	E 4 61
Blenheim Av.	D 6 65
Blenheim Gro.	C 7 64
Blenheim Rd.	D 7 65
Bloemfontein St., Cud.	J 3 63
Blucher St.	D 6 65
Blundell Ct.	G 4 62
Blythe Clo.	D 2 60
Bodmin Ct.	F 5 66
Bond Rd.	C 5 64
Borrowdale Clo.	J 7 67
Boundary St.	F 7 66
Bow St., Cud.	J 3 63
Bradbury St.	C 6 64
Bramcote Av.	D 2 60
Branksome Av.	C 6 64
Bratton Vw., Cud.	J 3 63
Bridge Gdns.	D 5 65
Bridge St.	D 5 65
Bridge St.	G 7 66
Brierfield Clo.	C 5 64
Bright St.	E 4 61
Brinckman St.	E 7 65
Britannia Clo.	D 6 65
Broadway	B 6 64
Broadway Ct.	B 6 64
Daleswood Av.	
BrontClo.	F 5 66
Brook Vale	G 5 66
Brookfield Ter.	G 2 62
Springbank Clo.	
Broomfield Clo.	B 7 64
Browning Clo.	F 4 61
Brunswick Clo.	E 3 61
Buckden Rd.	D 6 65
Prospect St.	
Buckley Ct.	D 7 65
Bude Ct.	F 5 66
Bungalows, The, Cud.	K 4 63
Burleigh St.	D 6 65
Burlington Arc.	D 6 65
Eldon St.	
Burn Pl.	D 2 60
Burton Av.	G 4 62
Burton Bank Rd.	E 4 61
Burton Cres.	G 3 62
Burton Rd.	E 5 65
Burton Rd.	H 3 62
Burton St.	D 5 65
Buttermere Way	J 7 67
Cumberland Dr.	
Buxton St.	E 3 61
Byath La., Cud.	K 3 63
Byland Way	G 5 66
Byron Dr.	F 4 61
Caistor Av.	C 7 64
Calder Cres.	G 7 66
Caldwell Clo., Cud.	K 2 63
California Cres.	D 7 65
California Gdns.	D 7 65
California St.	D 7 65
California Ter.	D 7 65
Cambourne Way	F 5 66
Canada St.	D 7 65
Canons Way	G 5 66
Carbis Clo.	F 5 66
Carey Av.	E 6 65
Carlton Rd.	F 2 61
Carlton St.	D 4 60
Carlton St., Cud.	J 2 63
Carnforth Rd.	G 4 62
Carr St.	G 4 62
Carrington Av.	D 4 60
Carrington St.	C 5 64
Carrs La., Cud.	K 4 63
Carrwood Rd.	G 6 66
Cartmel Ct.	G 3 62
Castle Row	F 5 66
Castle St.	D 7 65
Castlereagh St.	D 6 65
Cavendish Rd.	D 5 65
Cawley Pl.	E 4 61
Caxton St.	D 5 65
Cayton Clo.	D 2 60
Cedar Cres.	F 7 66
Cemetery Rd.	E 7 65
Chancel Way	G 5 66
Chapel Pl.	H 7 67
Chapel Sq.	D 7 65
Chapel St.	F 4 61
Chapel St.	H 7 67
Chapter Way	G 5 66
Charity St.	H 3 62
Charles St.	D 7 65
Charles St., Cud.	K 2 63
Charter Arc.	D 6 65
Cheapside	
Chatsworth Rd.	E 3 61
Cheapside	D 6 65
Cherry Clo., Cud.	K 2 63
Cherry Rd.	G 6 66
Chestnut Cres.	F 7 66
Cheviot Wk.	B 5 64
Chiltern Wk.	B 5 64
Chilton St.	E 7 65
Church Gro.	F 4 61
Church La.	D 5 65
Church St.	D 5 65
Church St.	G 4 62
Church St., Cud.	K 3 63
Church St., Gaw.	B 5 64
Church Vw.	C 5 64
Church Vw., Cud.	K 3 63
Churchfield Av., Cud.	K 3 63
Churchfield Cres., Cud.	K 3 63
Churchfield St.	D 6 65
Churchfield Ter., Cud.	K 3 63
Clanricarde St.	D 4 60
Clarence Rd.	F 4 61
Clarendon St.	D 6 65
Clarke St.	C 5 64
Claycliffe Ter.	C 7 64
Cranbrook St.	
Cleveland Ter.	D 2 60
Cliff Ter.	E 6 65
Cliffe Ct.	F 5 66
Cliffe La.	F 5 66
Clifton St.	E 7 65
Clipstone Av.	E 2 61
Clipstone Sq.	E 2 61

113

Street	Ref		Street	Ref		Street	Ref
Industry Rd.	F 2 61		Locke St.	C 7 64		Myrtle St.	C 6 64
Ingleton Wk.	C 6 64		Lockeaflash Cres.	G 7 66		Nelson Av.	E 4 61
Summer St.			Lockwood La.	D 7 65		Nelson St.	D 6 65
Intake La., Cud.	K 2 63		Long Row	E 4 61		Neville Av.	G 7 66
Intake La., Gaw.	B 5 64		Longcar La.	C 7 64		Neville Cres.	G 7 66
Issott St.	D 5 65		Longcar St.	C 6 64		New Hall La.	J 7 67
Jackson St., Cud.	J 3 63		Longcauseway	G 5 66		New Lodge Cres.	D 2 60
Jacques Row	G 5 66		Longman Rd.	D 5 65		New Lodge Estate	D 3 60
James St.	E 5 65		Longridge Rd.	G 3 62		New St.	D 6 65
Jenny La., Cud.	J 3 63		Lonsdale Av.	J 7 67		New St., Stairfoot	H 7 67
John St.	D 6 65		Lord St.	F 6 66		Newdale Av., Cud.	J 3 63
Johnson St.	C 6 64		Lower Thomas St.	D 6 65		Newfield Av.	G 4 62
Joseph St.	D 6 65		Loxley Rd.	H 5 67		Newhill Rd.	E 4 61
Judy Row	F 4 61		Lulworth Clo.	F 7 66		Newland Av., Cud.	J 3 63
Junction St.	E 7 65		Lund Av.	H 5 67		Newland Rd.	D 2 60
Kaye St.	D 5 65		Lund Cres.	H 5 67		Newlyn Dr.	F 5 66
Old Mill La.			Lund La.	H 5 67		Newstead Rd.	D 2 60
Kays Ter.	G 7 66		Lunn Rd., Cud.	J 3 63		Newton St.	C 6 64
Keir St.	C 6 64		Lytham Av.	G 3 62		Newtown Av., Cud.	J 3 63
Kelsey St.	E 7 65		Malcolm Clo.	G 7 66		Newtown Grn., Cud.	J 3 63
Kendal Gro.	J 7 67		*Reginald Rd.*			Nicholas St.	C 6 64
Kensington Rd.	C 5 64		Malham Ct.	C 6 64		*Lancaster St.*	
Kenton Wk., Gaw.	B 5 64		*Summer St.*			Nithdale Pl., Gaw.	B 5 64
Kenwood Clo.	G 7 66		Mallory Way, Cud.	K 2 63		Norfolk Clo.	F 4 61
Doncaster Rd.			Malthouse La.	E 6 65		Norman Clo.	G 4 62
Kenworthy Rd.	D 7 65		Malton Pl.	D 2 60		North Gate	C 4 60
Keresforth Hall Rd.	C 7 64		Malvern Clo.	B 5 64		North Pl.	B 5 64
Keswick Wk.	J 7 67		Manor Gdns.	J 7 67		Northumberland Way	H 6 67
Ketton Wk.	B 5 64		Manor Rd., Cud.	J 3 63		Nottingham Clo.	J 7 67
Kilnsea Wk.	D 6 65		Manor St.	G 2 62		Nursery Gdns.	G 7 66
Fitzwilliam St.			Mansfield Rd.	E 2 61		Nurseryday St.	D 7 65
King Edward St.	G 3 62		Maple Clo.	F 7 66		Oak Park Rd.	E 7 65
King Edwards Gdns.	D 7 65		Mark St.	D 6 65		Oak St.	C 6 64
Blenheim Rd.			Market Hill	D 6 65		Oakfield Wk.	B 5 64
King St.	E 6 65		Market Pl., Cud.	K 2 63		Oakham Pl.	B 5 64
Kingsley Clo.	E 3 61		Market St.	D 6 65		Oaklands Av.	G 4 62
Kingstone Pl.	C 7 64		Market St., Cud.	K 2 63		Oaks Cres.	F 7 66
Kinson St.	E 7 65		Marlborough Ter.	D 7 65		Oaks La.	F 6 66
Kirk Way	G 5 66		*Blenheim Rd.*			Oakwell La.	E 6 65
Kirkby Rd.	E 2 61		Marrick Clo., Gaw.	B 5 64		Oakwell Ter.	E 6 65
Kirkham Clo.	G 5 66		Marston Cres.	D 3 60		Old Mill La.	D 5 65
Kirkham Pl.	G 3 62		Martin Rd.	H 5 67		Old Rd.	E 4 61
Kirkstall Rd.	D 2 60		Mary Ann Clo.	G 5 66		Orchard Clo.	F 4 61
Kitson Dr.	G 5 66		Marys Gate	D 6 65		Orchard Wk.	D 5 65
Knowsley St.	C 6 64		Marys Pl.	B 5 64		Oriel Way	G 5 66
Laceby Ct.	C 7 64		Matlock Rd.	E 3 61		Osborne Ct.	G 4 62
Ladock Clo.	F 5 66		May Day Grn.	D 6 65		*Burton Rd.*	
Laithes Clo.	F 2 61		May Day Gro.	D 6 65		Osborne St.	E 7 65
Laithes Cres.	D 2 60		May Ter.	C 6 64		Oulton Dr., Cud.	K 2 63
Laithes La.	E 2 61		Mayfield	F 4 61		Oxford Pl.	H 7 67
Lamb La.	F 4 61		Meadow Av., Cud.	K 4 63		Oxford St.	E 7 65
Lambert Rd.	F 7 66		Meadow Dr.	G 4 62		Oxford St., Stairfoot	H 7 67
Lambra Rd.	D 6 65		Meadow St.	E 5 65		Oxleys Ter.	F 4 61
Lancaster Gate	D 6 65		Melrose Way	G 5 66		Oxton Rd.	E 2 61
St. Marys Pl.			Melvinia Cres.	C 4 60		Pall Mall	D 6 65
Lancaster St.	C 6 64		Mendip Clo.	B 5 64		Palm St.	C 5 64
Lang Av.	H 5 67		Methley St., Cud.	K 3 63		Parish Way	G 5 66
Langdale Rd.	E 6 65		Michael Rd.	H 5 67		Park Av.	D 2 60
Langdon Wk.	D 6 65		Middle Burn Clo.	E 7 65		Park Av.	D 6 65
Summer St.			Middlesex St.	D 7 65		*Park Gro.*	
Langsett Rd.	D 2 60		Midland St.	D 6 65		Park Av., Cud.	J 2 63
Lanton Way	F 5 66		Midland Ter.	H 4 62		Park Gro.	D 7 65
Larchfield Pl.	G 4 62		Milden Pl.	E 7 65		Park Rd.	C 7 64
Laurel Av.	G 7 66		Mill Hill La.	G 2 62		Park Row	D 6 65
Laxton Rd.	D 2 60		Milne St.	E 7 65		Park St.	D 7 65
Lea Rd.	F 3 61		Milton St.	E 5 65		Park Vw.	C 7 64
Ledbury Rd.	E 3 61		Minster Way	G 5 66		Parker St.	C 6 64
Leopold St.	C 6 64		Mona St.	D 5 65		Peak Rd.	E 2 61
Leslie Rd.	G 7 66		*Summer La.*			Peel Pl.	E 4 61
Lewis Rd.	H 4 62		Monk Ter.	H 4 62		Peel Sq.	D 6 65
Lime Tree Clo., Cud.	K 2 63		Monks Way	G 5 66		Peel St.	E 6 65
Willow Clo.			Monsal Cres.	E 2 61		Peel St., Wor.Com.	D 7 65
Limes Av., Gaw.	B 5 64		Montague St., Cud.	K 2 63		Penhill Clo., Gaw.	B 5 64
Limes Way	B 5 64		Moor Green Clo.	B 6 64		Pennine Way	B 5 64
Lindales, The	B 5 64		Moorland Av.	B 6 64		Penrhyn Wk.	J 6 67
Lindhurst Rd.	D 2 60		Moorland Ter., Cud.	K 4 63		Penrith Gro.	H 7 67
Lingard St.	C 5 64		Morton Pl.	G 4 62		Perseverance St.	C 6 64
Linton Clo.	B 6 64		Mottram St.	E 5 65		Peveril Cres.	E 2 61
Littleworth La.	G 5 66		Mount Clo.	D 7 65		Philip Rd.	G 7 66
Litton Wk.	C 6 64		Mount St.	D 6 65		Pike Lowe Gro., Map.	C 2 60
Summer St.			Mount St., Stairfoot	H 7 67		*Cloverlands Dr.*	
Livingstone Cres.	F 4 61		Mount Vernon Av.	E 7 65		Pinchall Dr.	G 4 62
Livingstone Ter.	D 6 65		Mucky La.	J 6 67		Pindar Oaks St.	E 7 65
Locke Av.	D 7 65		Murdoch Clo.	D 2 60		Pindar St.	E 7 65

Name	Ref		Name	Ref		Name	Ref
Pinfold Clo.	H 7 67		Rose Tree Ct., Cud.	J 2 63		Silverstone Av., Cud.	K 2 63
Pit La.	G 4 62		*Sycamore Av.*			Smithies La.	D 4 60
Pitt St.	D 6 65		Roseberry St.	G 7 66		Smithies St.	D 4 60
Pitt St. W.	D 6 65		Roseberry Ter.	E 6 65		Snetterton Clo., Cud.	K 2 63
Pleasant View St.	D 4 60		*Brinckman St.*			Snowdrop Ter.	E 6 65
Pleasant Vw., Cud.	K 4 63		Rosedale Gdns.	C 6 64		Somerset St.	D 6 65
Plumber St.	D 6 65		Rotherham Rd.	E 3 61		*Summer La.*	
Pogmoor La.	B 6 64		Rowan Dr., Gaw.	B 5 64		South Pl.	B 5 64
Pogmoor Rd.	B 6 64		Rowland Rd.	B 5 64		South St.	C 6 64
Pollitt St.	D 5 65		Royal St.	D 6 65		Southfield Rd., Cud.	K 4 63
Pond St.	D 7 65		Royd Av., Cud.	K 3 63		Southgate	C 5 64
Pontefract Rd.	H 4 62		Rufford Av.	E 2 61		Southwell St.	C 5 64
Pontefract Rd., Cud.	K 2 63		Russell Clo.	F 4 61		Spencer St.	D 7 65
Poplars Rd.	F 5 66		Rutland Way	B 5 64		Spring Gdns.,	G 4 62
Portier Av.	B 7 64		Rydal Ter.	E 6 65		Monk Bretton	
Portier Ter.	B 5 64		Rye Cft.	E 3 61		Spring St.	D 7 65
Portland St.	F 7 66		Sackville St.	D 6 65		Springfield Pl.	C 6 64
Poulton St.	G 3 62		Sadler Gate	D 6 65		*Dodworth Rd.*	
Preston Way	G 3 62		*St. Marys Pl.*			Springfield St.	C 6 64
Prince Arthur St.	C 5 64		St. Andrews Way	J 7 67		Springfield Ter.	C 6 64
Princess St.	D 6 65		St. Annes Dr.	G 3 62		Square, The	G 6 66
Priory Pl.	H 4 62		St. Bartholomews Ter.	E 7 65		Standhill Cres.	D 2 60
Priory Rd.	H 4 62		St. Catherines Way	B 6 64		Stanhope Gdns.	C 5 64
Prospect Rd.	J 3 63		St. Christopher Clo.	J 7 67		Stanhope St.	C 6 64
St. Johns Rd.			St. Clements Clo.	J 7 67		Stanley St.	C 6 64
Prospect St.	D 6 65		St. Davids Dr.	H 7 67		Stanley St., Cud.	K 4 63
Prospect St., Cud.	J 3 63		St. Edwards Av.	C 7 64		Stanton Clo.	D 3 60
Providence Ct.	D 7 65		St. Frances Boul.	G 2 62		Station Rd.	C 6 64
Providence Ct.	D 7 65		St. Georges Rd.	D 6 65		Station Rd., Cud.	H 4 62
Quaker La.	H 6 67		St. Helens Av.	F 3 61		Stocks La.	C 6 64
Quarry St.	E 6 65		St. Helens Boul	F 3 61		Stone St.	D 4 60
Quarry St.	K 3 63		St. Helens Vw.	F 4 61		Stonegarth Clo., Cud.	J 3 63
Queen St.	D 6 65		St. Helens Way	G 3 62		Stonehill Ri., Cud.	J 3 63
Queen St. S.	D 6 65		St. Helier Dr.	B 5 64		Strelly Rd.	D 2 60
Albert St.			St. Hilda Av.	B 6 64		Stretton Rd.	E 4 61
Queens Av.	C 5 64		St. Johns Rd.	D 7 65		Summer La.	C 5 64
Queens Dr.	C 5 64		St. Johns Rd., Cud.	J 3 63		Summer St.	C 6 64
Queens Gdns.	C 5 64		St. Leonards Way	J 7 67		Summerdale Rd., Cud.	J 3 63
Queens Rd.	D 6 65		St. Lukes Way	F 5 66		Sunderland Ter.	E 7 65
Queens Way	C 5 64		*St. Mathews Way*			Sunnybank Dr., Cud.	K 4 63
Race Common La.	D 7 65		St. Martins Clo.	B 6 64		Surrey Clo.	D 7 65
Race Common Rd.	C 7 64		St. Marys Pl.	D 6 65		Sutton Av.	D 2 60
Race St.	D 6 65		St. Mathews Way	F 5 66		Swanee Rd.	F 7 66
Radcliffe Rd.	E 2 61		St. Michaels Av.	G 3 62		Swift St.	C 5 64
Railway Cotts., Cud.	J 3 63		St. Owens Dr.	B 6 64		Sycamore Av., Cud.	J 2 63
Rainford Dr.	G 3 62		St. Pauls Par.	H 7 67		Sycamore St.	C 6 64
Raley St.	C 7 64		St. Peters Ter.	E 6 65		Sydney Ter.	E 7 65
Ravenfield Dr.	E 3 61		*Brinckman St.*			*Clifton St.*	
Raymond Rd.	G 7 66		Salisbury St.	C 5 64		Sykes Av.	C 5 64
Reasback Ter.	E 3 61		Samuel Rd., Gaw.	B 5 64		Sykes St.	C 7 64
Rebecca Row	D 7 65		Samuel Sq., Gaw.	B 5 64		Syndale Rd., Cud.	K 3 63
Rectory Way	G 5 66		Sandbeck Clo.	D 4 60		Tank Row	G 6 66
Red Brook Rd., Gaw.	B 5 64		Saville Ter.	D 7 65		Taylor Row	E 6 65
Redfearn St.	E 5 65		*Agnes Rd.*			Temple Way	G 5 66
Meadow St.			Saxon St., Cud.	K 3 63		Tennyson Rd.	F 4 61
Redhill Av.	F 7 66		Scar La.	H 7 67		Thirlmere Rd.	E 6 65
Regent Cres.	D 2 60		Scarfield Clo.	H 6 67		Thomas St.	D 6 65
Regent Gdns.	D 5 65		School Hill, Cud.	K 2 63		Thoresby Av.	F 5 66
Regent St.	D 6 65		*Market Pl.*			Thorne Clo.	D 2 60
Regent St. S.	D 6 65		School St.	C 5 64		Thornley Ter.	D 6 65
Reginald Rd.	G 7 66		School St., Cud.	K 2 63		Thornton Rd.	F 7 66
Rhodes Ter.	E 7 65		School St., Stairfoot	G 7 66		Thornton Ter.	F 7 66
Gold St.			Selby Rd.	D 3 60		Thorntree La.	C 5 64
Riber Av.	E 2 61		Sennen Cft.	F 5 66		*Greenfoot La.*	
Richard Av.	E 3 61		Seth St.	E 6 65		Thruxton Clo., Cud.	K 2 63
Richard Rd.	E 3 61		Seth Ter., Map.	C 2 60		Tippit La., Cud.	K 3 63
Richard St.	D 6 65		Shaftesbury St.	G 7 66		Top Fold	J 7 67
Plumber St.			Shambles St.	D 6 65		Top Row	J 7 67
Richmond St.	C 6 64		Shaw La.	C 6 64		Topcliffe Rd.	E 4 61
Dean St.			Shaw St.	C 6 64		Tor Clo.	E 4 61
Ridings Av.	E 3 61		Shawfield Rd.	G 3 62		*Rotherham Rd.*	
Ridings, The	F 4 61		Sheaf Ct.	G 7 66		Totley Clo.	F 2 61
Roberts Av.	E 3 61		Sheffield Rd.	E 7 65		Tower St.	D 7 65
Roberts St., Cud.	J 3 63		Shelley Dr.	F 5 66		Town End	D 6 65
Roche Clo.	F 5 66		Shepherd St.	D 6 65		Tredis Clo.	F 5 66
Rochester Rd.	F 4 61		Sherburn Rd.	D 2 60		Treecrest Ri.	D 4 60
Rock St.	C 6 64		Sheridan Ct.	F 5 66		Treelands, Gaw.	B 5 64
Rock Ter.	F 5 66		Sherwood St.	E 6 65		Trewan Ct.	F 5 66
Rockingham St.	D 4 60		Shirland Av.	E 3 61		Trowell Way	E 2 61
Rodney Ter.	E 6 65		Short Row	E 4 61		Trueman Ter.	H 5 67
Roehampton Ri.	H 7 67		Sidcop Rd., Cud.	J 2 63		Truro Ct.	F 5 66
Roger Rd.	H 5 67		Silver St.	D 6 65		*Sennen Cft.*	
Rose Av.	E 3 61		Silverdale Dr.,	G 4 62		Tumbling La.	H 3 62
Rose Tree Av., Cud.	J 2 63		Monk Bretton			Tune St.	E 7 65

117

NOTES

NOTES

DONCASTER

District Abbreviations

Ark.	Arksey	Can.	Cantley	Nut.	Nutwell	Sprot.	Sprotborough
Arm.	Armthorpe	Eden.	Edenthorpe	Scaws.	Scawsby	War.	Warmsworth
Ben.	Bentley	Newt.	Newton	Scawth.	Scawthorpe		

Abbey Wk., Scaws.	C 4 68	Bainbridge Rd.	D 6 73	Broadway, The	C 8 72
Abbott St.	D 6 73	Balby Carr Bank	E 7 73	Brockhole Clo.	J 7 75
Abercorn Rd.	H 5 71	Balby Rd.	D 7 73	Brompton Rd., Sprot.	B 6 72
Abingdon Rd.	G 4 70	Baldwin Av., Ben.	D 4 69	Bront Av.	C 8 72
Acacia Av.	J 7 75	Balmoral Rd.	F 5 70	Brooke St.	E 4 69
Adlard Rd.	G 4 70	Bank Side	E 6 73	Broom Hill Dr.	J 7 75
Aintree Av.	H 6 75	Bank St.	E 6 73	Broughton Av., Ben.	D 3 69
Aintree Clo.,	B 4 68	Bardolf Rd.	J 7 75	Broughton Rd.	H 8 75
Scaws.		Barnby Dun Rd.	H 3 71	Browning Av.	D 8 73
Albany Rd.	D 7 73	Barnsley Rd.,	B 3 68	Broxholme La.	E 5 69
Albion Pl.	F 5 70	Scaws.		Bruce Cres.	G 4 70
Albion Ter.	D 6 73	Barnstone St.	D 6 73	Brunel Rd.	D 4 69
Aldam Rd.	C 8 72	Barrel La.	B 8 72	Buckingham Rd.	F 5 70
Alder Gro.	C 7 72	Barret Rd.	J 6 75	Bude Rd.	D 7 73
Alderson Dr.	F 6 74	Barrie Rd.	D 8 73	Burden Clo.	E 6 73
Aldesworth Rd.	J 6 75	Basil Av., Arm.	J 3 71	Burford Av.	C 8 72
Alexandra Rd.	D 7 73	Baxter Av.	F 5 70	Burnham Clo.	G 7 74
Allendale Rd., Ben.	C 5 68	Baxter Gate	E 5 69	Burnham Gro.,	C 3 68
Allerton St.	E 5 69	Beaconsfield Rd.	D 6 73	Scawth.	
Almond Rd.	J 7 75	Beaufort Rd.	G 5 70	Burns Rd.	D 8 73
Alston Clo.	H 7 75	Beckett Rd.	F 5 70	Burton Av.	D 7 73
Alston Rd.	H 8 75	Bedale Rd.	B 3 68	Burton Ter.	D 7 73
Alwyn Av.,	C 3 68	Sunnyfields		Busley Gdns.	D 3 69
Scawth.		Beech Gro., Ben.	D 3 69	Byron Av.	C 5 68
Amersall Cres.,	C 3 68	Beech Gro., War.	B 8 72	Byron Av.	D 8 73
Scawth.		Beechcroft Rd.	C 8 72	Cambria Dr.	C 8 72
Amersall Rd.,	C 3 68	Beechfield Rd.	E 6 73	Camden Pl.	E 6 73
Scawth.		Belle Vue Av.	G 6 74	Canterbury Clo.,	C 4 68
Anchorage Cres.	D 5 69	Bellis Av.	D 7 73	Scaws.	
Ben.		Belmont Av.	E 6 73	Canterbury Rd.	F 4 70
Anchorage La., Ben.	C 4 68	Belvedere	C 8 72	Cantley La.	H 6 75
Anelay Rd.	C 7 72	Bennetthorpe	F 6 74	Or Sand Rd.	
Anfield Rd.	J 7 75	Bentinck Clo.	E 6 73	Cantley Manor Av.	J 7 75
Ansten Cres.	J 7 75	Bentley Av.	D 6 73	Cantley Riding	J 4 71
Ansten Gdns.	J 7 75	Bentley Common La.,	E 3 69	Cardigan Rd.	H 4 71
Apley Rd.	E 6 73	Ben.		Carisbrooke Rd.	G 5 70
Apostle Clo.	C 8 72	Bentley Rd., Ben.	D 3 69	Carlisle Rd.	G 3 70
Appleby Rd.	H 5 71	Berwick Way	H 4 71	Carlton Rd.	F 4 70
Appleton Way, Ben.	D 3 69	Bessacarr La.	J 8 75	Carr Hill	D 7 73
Ardeen Rd.	G 5 70	Beverley Gdns.	B 4 68	Carr House Rd.	E 6 73
Argyle Av.	G 4 70	Beverley Rd.	G 4 70	Carr La.	J 8 75
Arklow Rd.	G 4 70	Bewicke Av., Scaws.	B 4 68	Carr La., Hyde Park	E 6 73
Arkwright Rd.	D 4 69	Birch Rd.	J 7 75	Carr View Av.	D 7 73
Armitage Rd.	C 7 72	Birchen Clo.	J 8 75	Castell Cres.	J 6 75
Armthorpe Rd.	G 4 70	Black Bank	F 6 74	Castle Clo., Newt.	C 6 72
Arundel Gdns.,	C 3 68	Blackwood Av.	C 8 72	Catherine St.	E 6 73
Scawth.		Blake Av.	F 4 70	Cecil Av., War.	B 8 72
Ascot Av.	H 6 75	Blundell Clo.	J 7 75	Cedar Rd.	C 8 72
Ascot Dr.	B 4 68	Bolton Hill Rd.	J 8 75	Central Av., Ben.	D 3 69
Ashburnham Gdns.	C 5 68	Bolton Wind	J 8 75	Central Boulevard	G 4 70
Ben.		Bond Clo.	E 6 73	Chadwick Rd., Ben.	D 4 69
Ashdale Rd.	B 8 72	Boswell Rd.	H 7 75	Challenger Dr.	C 5 68
Ashdown Pl.,	C 3 68	Boundary Av.	H 3 71	Chamberlain Av.,	D 4 69
Scawth.		Bowers Fold	E 5 69	Ben.	
Ashfield Rd.	D 7 73	Pedestrian Wk.		Chancery Pl.	E 5 69
Askrigg Clo.	J 7 75	Bowlease Gdns.	H 7 75	Duke St.	
Atholl Cres.	H 4 71	Bradford Rd.	H 3 71	Chapel St.	D 6 73
Athron St.	E 5 69	Bradford Row	E 5 69	Chappell Dr.	E 5 69
Auckland Rd.	F 4 70	Pedestrian Wk.		Charles Cres., Arm.	J 4 71
Austen Av.	C 8 72	Braemar Rd.	G 5 70	Charles St.	E 4 69
Austerfield Av.,	D 3 69	Bramham Rd.	J 6 75	Charnwood Dr.	C 8 72
Ben.		Bramworth Rd.	C 6 72	Chatsworth Cres.	C 3 68
Avenue Rd.	F 4 70	Brancroft Clo.	H 8 75	Scawth.	
Avenue, The	H 6 75	Brantwood Cres.	J 6 75	Checkstone Av.	J 8 75
Aviemore Rd., War.	C 8 72	Bretby Clo.	J 8 75	Chelmsford Dr.	F 4 70
Avoca Av.	G 5 70	Breydon Av., Scaws.	C 4 68	Cheltenham Rd.	H 4 71
Avondale Rd.	G 5 70	Bridge Gro., Ben.	C 4 68	Cheltenham Ri.	B 4 68
Axholme Rd.	F 4 70	Bridge Rd.	H 7 75	Chepstow Gdns.,	B 4 68
Aylesbury Rd.	G 5 70	Bridge St.	D 6 73	Scaws.	
Ayresome Wk.	J 7 75	Bridge Ter.	D 6 73	Chequer Av.	F 6 74
Aysgarth Clo.	J 7 75	Brierley Rd.	H 7 75	Chequer Rd.	E 6 73
Back La., Ben.	B 4 68	Bristol Gro.	G 4 70	Cherry La.	D 5 69
Backside La.	B 8 72	Broach Gate,	C 3 68	Cherry Tree Rd.	D 6 73
Badsworth Rd., War.	B 8 72	Scawth.		Cheshire Rd.	E 4 69
Bahram Rd.	H 7 75	Broad Wk., Sprot.	B 7 72	Chester Rd.	F 4 70

120

Chesterton Rd.	E 8	73
Chestnut Av.	G 3	70
Cheswold Rd.	E 5	69
Cheviot Dr.,	C 3	68
Scawth.		
Childers St.	F 6	74
Chiltern Rd.,	C 3	68
Scawth.		
Christ Church Rd.	E 5	69
Church Cottage Ms.	C 7	72
Church La., Balby	C 7	72
Church La., Can.	J 8	75
Church St.	E 5	69
Church St.	J 7	75
Church St., Ben.	D 3	69
Church Vw.	E 5	69
Church Way	E 5	69
Churchfield Clo.	D 3	69
Churchill Av., Ben.	D 4	69
Churchill Rd.	F 4	70
Clarell Gdns.	J 6	75
Clarence Av.	D 7	73
Clark Av.	F 6	74
Clayworth Dr.	D 7	73
Cleveland St.	E 6	73
Clifton Cres.	G 4	70
Clifton Dr., Newt.	C 6	72
Clumber Rd.	F 6	74
Colchester Ct.,	C 4	68
Scaws.		
Coldstream Av., War.	B 8	72
College Rd.	E 6	73
Common La., War.	B 8	72
Coniston Pl.	C 3	68
Scawth.		
Coniston Rd.	H 5	71
Convent Gro.	H 7	75
Conyers Rd., Ben.	D 4	69
Cooke St., Ben.	D 3	69
Cookson St.	D 7	73
Cooper St.	F 6	74
Coopers Ter.	E 5	69
Copley Cres., Scaws.	B 4	68
Copley Rd.	E 5	69
Cornwall Rd.	G 4	70
Coronation Gdns.,	B 8	72
War.		
Coronation Rd.	D 7	73
Coterel Cres.	J 6	75
Cotswold Gdns.,	C 3	68
Scawth.		
Court Clo.	B 4	68
Nottingham Clo.		
Court Clo.	B 4	68
St. Patricks Way		
Coventry Gro.	C 3	68
Craigholme Cres.	H 3	71
Craithie Rd.	F 5	70
Cranbrook Rd.	F 4	70
Craven Clo.	J 7	75
Crawshaw Rd.	D 6	73
Crecy Av.	H 5	71
Crimpsall Rd.	D 6	73
Crochley Clo.	J 6	75
Croft Rd.	C 8	72
Cromer Rd.	H 5	71
Crompton Av., Ben.	C 5	68
Crompton Rd.	G 3	70
Cromwell Dr.,	C 6	72
Newt.		
Cromwell Rd., Ben.	D 4	69
Crookes Rd.	D 8	73
Cross Bank	D 7	73
Cross Gate, Ben.	D 4	69
Cross Riding	J 5	71
Cross St.	D 7	73
Crossland Way,	C 3	68
Scawth.		
Crossleigh Gro.,	D 3	69
Ben.		
Crossways	G 3	70
Crossways N.	G 3	70
Crossways S.	G 4	70
Crusader Dr.	C 5	68

Cumberland Av.	G 5	70
Cunningham Rd.	E 6	73
Cusworth La.,	C 4	68
Scaws.		
Cusworth Rd., Ben.	D 3	69
Danum Rd.	F 6	74
Dargle Rd.	G 4	70
Darrington Dr.,	B 8	72
War.		
Dean Clo.	B 6	72
Decoy Bank	E 6	73
Dell Cres.	C 6	72
Denison Rd.	D 6	73
Derby Rd.	H 3	71
Devonshire Rd.	G 4	70
Dirleton Dr., War.	B 8	72
Dixon Cres.	C 7	72
Dockin Hill Rd.	E 5	69
Don St.	E 4	69
Doncaster By-pass	B 5	68
Doncaster Rd., Arm.	J 4	71
Dorset Cres.	H 4	71
Douglas Rd.	C 7	72
Drake Rd.	F 4	70
Drummond Av.,	B 3	68
Sunnyfields		
Dryden Rd.	E 8	73
Dublin Rd.	G 4	70
Dudley Rd.	G 5	70
Duke St.	E 5	69
Dundas St.	F 4	70
Dunleary Rd.	G 5	70
Dunniwood Av.	J 8	75
Durham Rd.	F 3	70
Durnford Rd.	F 4	70
Earlesmere Av.	D 7	73
Earlston Dr., Ben.	D 4	69
East Laith Gate	E 5	69
East St.	E 6	73
Eden Gro.	D 6	73
Edgehill Rd.	H 3	71
Edith Ter., Scawth.	C 3	68
Edward St., Arm.	J 3	71
Ellerker Av.	D 6	73
Ellers Av.	H 7	75
Ellers Cres.	H 7	75
Ellers Dr.	H 7	75
Ellers Rd.	G 7	74
Ellerton Gdns.	H 6	75
Elmfield Rd.	E 6	73
Elmham Rd.	J 6	75
Elsworth Clo.	E 6	73
Elwis St.	D 5	69
Ely Rd.	F 3	70
Emley Dr.,	B 3	68
Sunnyfields		
Endcliffe Way	H 3	71
Ennerdale Rd.	H 4	71
Ennis Cres.	G 4	70
Epsom Rd.	H 6	75
Eskdale Dr.,	C 3	68
Scawth.		
Eskdale Wk.,	B 3	68
Sunnyfields		
Essex Av.	G 5	70
Evanston Gdns.	D 7	73
Evelyn Av.	G 5	70
Everingham Rd.	J 6	75
Ewood Dr.	J 7	75
Exchange St.	E 6	73
Exeter Rd.	G 4	70
Factory La.	E 5	69
Fairfax Rd.	G 5	70
Fairfield Clo.	H 8	75
Fairfield Rd., Ben.	C 4	68
Farndale Rd.	C 3	68
Sunnyfields		
Fern Av., Ben.	D 3	69
Fern Clo.	H 4	71
Fernhurst Rd.	H 4	71
Ferrers Rd.	F 4	70
Filby Rd., Scaws.	C 4	68
Finch Rd.	C 8	72
Finkle St., Ben.	D 3	69

Firbeck Rd.	F 6	74
Firth St.	D 6	73
Fisher Ter., Ben.	D 4	69
Flint Rd.	H 4	71
Florence Av.	D 7	73
Flowitt St.	D 6	73
Forehill Av.	H 8	75
Forest Ri.	C 8	72
Forster Rd.	D 8	73
Fossard Clo.	G 3	70
Foundry Rd.	D 6	73
Fowler Bridge Rd.,	E 3	69
Ben.		
Frances St.	E 5	69
Frank Rd., Ben.	D 4	69
Franklin Cres.	F 5	70
French Gate	E 5	69
Friars Gate	E 5	69
Furnivall Rd.	D 7	73
Galsworthy Clo.	C 8	72
Garden Ter., Ben.	D 3	69
Gardens La.	C 6	72
Gayton Clo.	D 8	73
George St., Arm.	J 3	71
Gifford Dr., War.	B 8	72
Gilberthorpe Rd.	C 7	72
Gill St.	E 6	73
Gladstone Rd.	D 6	73
Glamis Rd.	G 5	70
Glastonbury Gate,	B 4	68
Scaws.		
Glebe St., War.	B 8	72
Glenfield Rd.	D 6	73
Gloucester Rd.	G 4	70
Glyn Av.	E 5	69
Goldsborough Rd.	G 5	70
Goldsmith Rd.	E 8	73
Goodison Boulevard	J 7	75
Goodwood Gdns.	H 6	75
Gordon St.	E 5	69
Granby Cres.	F 6	74
Grange Av.	D 7	73
Grange Clo.	J 8	75
Grange Rd.	J 8	75
Grasmere Av.	H 5	71
Gray Gdns.	D 8	73
Great Central Av.	D 7	73
Green Boulevard	J 7	75
Green Dyke La.	E 6	73
Green Field La.	D 6	73
Green St.	C 8	72
Greenhouse Rd.	G 4	70
Greenleafe Av.	H 3	71
Grenville Rd.	C 8	72
Greyfriars Rd.	E 5	69
Grice Clo.	J 6	75
Grosvenor Cres.,	B 8	72
War.		
Grosvenor Ter.	B 8	72
Grosvenor Cres.		
Grove Av., Ben.	D 4	69
Grove Hill Rd.	H 3	71
Grove Pl.	E 6	73
Grove Vale	H 3	71
Grove, The	G 4	70
Guest La., War.	B 7	72
Guildford Rd.	G 3	70
Gullane Dr., War.	B 8	72
Gurney Rd.	D 8	73
Haigh Rd.	D 7	73
Hake Hill Clo.	H 8	75
Halifax Cres., Ben.	C 4	68
Hall Croft Hill	F 5	70
Hall Flatt La.	C 7	72
Hall Gate	E 5	69
Hallam Clo.	H 7	75
Halmshaw Ter., Ben.	D 3	69
Hamilton Clo.	F 6	74
Hamilton Park Rd.	B 4	68
Hamilton Rd.	F 6	74
Hampton Rd.	F 5	70
Harcourt Clo.	H 7	75
Hardy Rd.	F 4	70
Harewood Rd.	G 5	70

122

Newstead Rd., Scawth.	C 3 68	
Newton Dr., Ben.	C 5 68	
Newton La., Ben.	C 5 68	
Nicholson Rd.	D 6 73	
Ninian Gro.	J 7 75	
Norborough Rd.	F 4 70	
Norbreck Clo., War.	B 8 72	
Norbreck Rd., War.	B 8 72	
Norfolk Rd.	D 8 73	
Norman Cres., Scawth.	B 3 68	
North Bridge Rd.	D 5 69	
North St.	E 6 73	
North Wall	E 5 69	
Trafford Way		
Northampton Rd.	G 4 70	
Northfield Av., Ben.	D 4 69	
Northfield Rd., Ben.	D 4 69	
Northumberland Av.	G 4 70	
Norton Rd.	G 4 70	
Norwich Rd.	G 3 70	
Norwith Rd.	J 8 75	
Nostell Pl.	H 8 75	
Nottingham Clo., Scaws.	B 4 68	
Nottingham St.	E 7 73	
Nutwell Clo.	J 8 75	
Oak Ter.	E 6 73	
Oakdale Rd.	B 8 72	
Oakhill Rd.	G 4 70	
Oaklands Dr.	H 7 75	
Oaklands Gdns.	H 7 75	
Oakwood Rd.	C 7 72	
Ogden Rd.	H 3 71	
Old Hall Clo., Sprot. Park	B 6 72	
Old Hall Cres., Ben.	D 3 69	
Old Hall Pl., Ben.	D 3 69	
Old Hall Rd., Ben.	D 3 69	
Old Hexthorpe	C 6 72	
Oliver Rd.	D 7 73	
Orchard St.	D 6 73	
Ormesby Cres., Scaws.	C 4 68	
Osborne Rd.	F 5 70	
Oswin Av.	D 7 73	
Oval, The	H 6 75	
Oversley Rd.	F 4 70	
Oxford Pl.	E 6 73	
Oxford St.	E 6 73	
Palington Gro.	J 6 75	
Palmer St.	F 6 74	
Pamela Dr., War.	B 8 72	
Park Av.	B 6 72	
Park Av., Arm.	J 3 71	
Park Clo.	B 6 72	
Park Cres., War.	B 8 72	
Park Dr., Sprot.	B 6 72	
Park La.	H 6 75	
Park Rd.	E 5 69	
Park Ter.	E 5 69	
Parkinson St.	E 4 69	
Parkstone Way	H 3 71	
Parkway N.	F 4 70	
Parkway S.	G 4 70	
Partridge Flatt Rd.	J 8 75	
Partridge Ri.	J 8 75	
Paxton Cres., Arm.	J 4 71	
Pearwood Cres.	C 8 72	
Pells Clo.	E 5 69	
Pembroke Av.	D 8 73	
Pembroke Ri., Scaws.	B 4 68	
Penistone St.	E 5 69	
Penrith Rd.	G 5 70	
Petersgate, Scawth.	C 3 68	
Peveril Rd.	C 8 72	
Pheasant Riding	J 4 71	
Piccadilly, Ben.	D 3 69	
Pilkington Rd.	F 7 74	
Pine Rd.	J 7 75	
Pinewood Av.	C 8 72	
Pipering La., Scawth.	C 3 68	

Plane Clo.	J 7 75	
Plumpton Park Rd.	J 8 75	
Plunkett Rd.	F 5 70	
Pond St.	E 6 73	
Poplar Dr.	H 4 71	
Poplar Ter., Ben.	D 3 69	
Priestley Clo.	C 8 72	
Prince Gate	E 5 69	
Princes Rd.	G 6 74	
Princes St.	E 5 69	
Printing Office St.	E 5 69	
Priory Pl.	E 5 69	
Quaker La., War.	B 8 72	
Queen St.	E 7 73	
Queens Ct., Ben.	D 4 69	
Queens Dr., Ben.	D 4 69	
Queens Gate	E 5 69	
Queens Rd.	F 5 70	
Queensberry Rd.	H 5 71	
Raby Rd.	F 4 70	
Radiance Rd.	F 4 70	
Radnor Way	H 4 71	
Rainton Rd.	F 6 74	
Raleigh Ter.	C 8 72	
Ramsay Cres., Ben.	D 4 69	
Ramsden Rd.	D 6 73	
Ranworth Clo., Scaws.	C 4 68	
Ranyard Rd.	C 7 72	
Ravensworth Rd.	F 6 74	
Rawson Clo.	J 6 75	
Raymond Rd., Ben.	C 4 68	
Rectory Gdns.	F 5 70	
Regent Gro., Ben.	C 4 68	
Regent Sq.	E 5 69	
Regent St.	D 7 73	
Richmond Hill Rd., Sprot.	C 6 72	
Richmond Rd., Sunnyfields	B 3 68	
Riley Av.	C 8 72	
Ripon Av.	F 4 70	
Riverdale Rd., Scawth.	C 3 68	
Riverside, Sprot. Park	B 6 72	
Riviera Mt.	D 4 69	
Riviera Par.	D 4 69	
Roberts Rd.	D 6 73	
Rochester Row, Scaws.	B 4 68	
Rockbridge Av., Broughton Av.	D 3 69	
Rockingham Rd.	F 4 70	
Rockley Nook	G 3 70	
Roehampton Ri., Scaws.	C 4 68	
Roman Rd.	F 6 74	
Roman Ridge, Scawth.	B 3 68	
Ronald Rd.	D 7 73	
Rose Av.	D 7 73	
Rose Cres., Ben.	C 3 68	
Rose Hill	H 6 75	
Rose Hill Ri.	H 6 75	
Rose Moor Gro.	H 6 75	
Rosedale Rd., Sunnyfields	B 3 68	
Rosegarth Clo., Scawth.	C 3 68	
Rotherwood Clo., Scaws.	B 4 68	
Rowan Ct.	H 4 71	
Rowan Garth, Ben.	D 4 69	
Rowan Mt.	G 4 70	
Rowena Dr., Scaws.	B 4 68	
Rowland Pl.	E 6 73	
Roxby Clo.	H 8 75	
Royal Av.	F 5 70	
Royston Av., Ben.	D 3 69	
Rufford Rd.	F 6 74	
Runnymeade Rd.	G 5 70	
Ruskin Av.	D 8 73	
Ruthven Dr., War.	B 7 72	
Rutland St.	F 5 70	

Rydal Pl., Scawth.	C 3 68	
Rydale Wk., Sunnyfields	B 3 68	
St. Agnes Rd.	G 6 74	
St. Andrews Ter.	E 6 73	
St. Annes Rd.	G 6 74	
St. Augustines Rd.	G 6 74	
St. Catherines Av.	D 7 73	
St. Cecilias Rd.	G 6 74	
St. Chads Way, Sprot. Park	B 6 72	
St. Christophers Cres., Scaws.	C 4 68	
St. Clements Clo. Scaws.	B 4 68	
St. Davids Dr., Scaws.	B 4 68	
St. Erics Rd.	H 7 75	
St. George Gate	E 5 69	
St. Georges Rd.	G 6 74	
St. Giles Gate, Scaws.	B 4 68	
St. Helens Rd.	G 6 74	
St. Hildas Rd.	G 6 74	
St. James Bri.	E 6 73	
St. James Gdns.	D 6 73	
St. James St.	E 6 73	
St. Johns Rd.	D 7 73	
St. Leonards Lea, Scaws.	C 4 68	
St. Margarets Rd.	G 6 74	
St. Martins Av.	C 4 68	
St. Marys Cres.	F 5 70	
St. Marys Rd.	F 4 70	
St. Michaels Rd.	G 6 74	
St. Patricks Rd.	G 5 70	
St. Patricks Way	B 4 68	
St. Davids Dr.		
St. Pauls Par., Scaws.	C 4 68	
St. Peters Rd.	C 7 72	
St. Sepulchre Gate	E 5 69	
St. Sepulchre Gate W.	E 6 73	
St. Swithins Ter.	E 6 73	
St. Thomass Clo.	C 8 72	
St. Ursulas Rd.	G 6 74	
St. Vincent Av.	F 5 70	
St. Vincent Rd.	F 5 70	
St. Wilfrids Ct.	J 7 75	
St. Wilfrids Rd.	H 6 75	
Salisbury Rd.	D 6 73	
Samuel St.	C 8 72	
Sand Rd. or Can. La.	H 6 75	
Sandal Park Dr.	H 3 71	
Sandall Beat La.	H 4 71	
Sandall Beat Rd.	H 5 71	
Sandall Ri.	G 4 70	
Sandbeck Rd.	F 6 74	
Sandcliffe Rd.	G 4 70	
Sandford Rd.	D 8 73	
Sandown Gdns.	H 6 75	
Sandringham Rd.	G 5 70	
Sandrock Dr.	J 8 75	
Sandy La.	G 6 74	
Saundy Clo.	H 7 75	
Saxton Av.	H 7 75	
Scaftworth Clo.	H 8 75	
Scarll Rd.	D 6 73	
Scarth Av.	D 7 73	
Scot La.	E 5 69	
Selby Rd.	G 4 70	
Selhurst Cres.	J 7 75	
Selkirk Av.	B 8 72	
Selkirk Rd.	H 4 71	
Senior Rd.	D 6 73	
Shady Side	D 6 73	
Shaftesbury Av.	G 5 70	
Shakespeare Av., Ben.	C 5 68	
Shardlow Gdns.	J 8 75	
Shaw La.	H 3 71	
Shay, The	J 7 75	
Sheardon St.	D 6 73	

123

Shelley Av.	D 8	73
Shelley Gro., Ben.	C 5	68
Sheppard Rd.	D 7	73
Sheridan Av.	E 8	73
Sherwood Av.,	B 4	68
Sunnyfields		
Sherwood Dr.	C 8	72
Shetland Gdns.	H 4	71
Shirburn Gdns.	J 6	75
Shirley Rd.	D 6	73
Short La.	G 7	74
Short Rd.	H 5	71
Shotton Wk.	E 6	73
Sidney Rd.	G 5	70
Silver Jubilee Clo.	H 4	71
Silver St.	E 5	69
Sincil Way	J 7	75
Sledmere Rd.,	C 4	68
Sunnyfields		
Smith Sq.	C 7	72
Smith St.	C 7	72
Society St.	E 5	69
Prince Gate		
Somersby Av., Ben.	C 5	68
Somerset Rd.	E 6	73
Somerton Dr.	J 7	75
South Par.	E 5	69
South St.	E 6	73
South Wall	E 5	69
Trafford Way		
Southwell Rd.	F 4	70
Spansyke St.	D 6	73
Spencer Av.	F 5	70
Spinney, The	C 8	72
Spring Gdns.	E 5	69
Springcroft Dr.,	C 3	68
Scawth.		
Springwell La.	C 8	72
Springwood Rd.,	C 3	68
Scawth.		
Sprotborough Rd.,	B 6	72
Ben.		
Stanhope Rd.	F 4	70
Stanley Gdns.	D 6	73
Stanley Rd., Scawth.	B 3	68
Stapleton Rd., War.	B 8	72
Station Approach	E 5	69
Trafford Way		
Stevens Rd.	D 6	73
Stevenson Rd.	D 8	73
Stewart St.	E 6	73
Stirling St.	E 6	73
Stockbridge Av.,	D 3	69
Ben.		
Broughton Av.		
Stockil Rd.	F 6	74
Stone Close Av.	D 6	73
Stone Font Gro.	J 7	75
Stonehill Ri.,	C 3	68
Scawth.		
Stoops La.	H 8	75
Stoops Rd.	H 7	75
Strafford Rd.	F 4	70
Strathmore Rd.	G 5	70
Sturton Clo.	H 8	75
Suffolk Rd.	D 8	73
Sunningdale Rd.	G 4	70
Sunny Bar	E 5	69
Surrey St.	D 7	73
Sussex St.	D 7	73
Sutton St.	D 6	73
Swaith Av., Scawth.	C 3	68

Swinburne Av.	D 8	73
Sycamore Gro.	J 7	75
Sylvester Av.	E 6	73
Symes Gdns.	J 6	75
Teeside Clo.	B 4	68
Telford Rd.	D 4	69
Ten Pound Wk.	E 7	73
Tenby Gdns.	D 7	73
Tennyson Av., Ben.	C 5	68
Tenter La., War.	B 8	72
Tenter Rd., War.	B 8	72
Thealby Gdns.	H 7	75
Thellusson Av.,	B 4	68
Scaws.		
Theobald Av.	F 6	74
Theobald Clo.	F 6	74
Thomson Av.	C 7	72
Thoresby Av.	F 6	74
Thorn Garth, Ben.	D 4	69
Thorne Rd.	E 5	69
Thornhill Av.	G 4	70
Thorntondale Rd.,	B 3	68
Sunnyfields		
Tickhill Rd.	D 8	73
Top Hall La.	J 8	75
Top Hall Rd.	J 8	75
Top La.	G 8	74
Torksey Clo.	J 8	75
Town End	D 4	69
Willow Bridge Rd.		
Town Field Villas	F 5	70
Town Moor Av.	F 5	70
Trafford Way	E 5	69
Tranmoor Av.	J 7	75
Travis Gdns.	C 6	72
Truro Av.	G 3	70
Tudor Rd.	G 5	70
Ullswater Wk.,	B 3	68
Sunnyfields		
Union St.	E 6	73
Urban Rd.	D 6	73
Valiant Gdns.	C 5	68
Vaughan Av.	E 5	69
Ventnor Clo.	C 7	72
Victoria Rd.	D 7	73
Victorian Cres.	F 5	70
Villa Park Rd.	J 7	75
Villas, The	D 6	73
Volunteer Yard	E 5	69
French Gdns.		
Wainwright Rd.	F 6	74
Wallace Rd.	C 8	72
Walpole Clo.	C 8	72
Walsham Dr., Scaws.	C 4	68
Warde Av.	C 8	72
Warmsworth Rd., War.	B 8	72
Warren Clo.	G 5	70
Warren La.	J 8	75
Warwick Rd.	G 4	70
Washington Gro.,	D 3	69
Ben.		
Watch House La.,	C 4	68
Ben.		
Waterdale	E 6	73
Waverley Av.	C 7	72
Welbeck Rd.	F 6	74
Wellcroft Rd.	H 4	71
Wellington Gro.,	D 3	69
Ben.		
Wells Rd.	F 4	70
Welton Clo.	H 8	75
Wembley Clo.	H 4	71

Wensley Cres.	J 7	75
Wensleydale Rd.	B 3	68
Wentworth Rd.	F 4	70
West Av.	D 7	73
West End Av., Ben.	D 3	69
West Gro.	G 4	70
West Laith Gate	E 5	69
West St.	E 5	69
West Wall	E 5	69
Trafford Way		
Westbourne Gdns.	C 8	72
Westerdale Rd.,	B 3	68
Sunnyfields		
Westfield Rd.	D 7	73
Westholme Rd.	D 6	73
Westminster Cres.	H 4	71
Westmorland St.	C 8	72
Weston Rd.	D 8	73
Wetherby Clo.	B 4	68
Wharf Rd.	E 4	69
Wharncliffe St.	D 6	73
Wheatley Hall Rd.	F 4	70
Whin Hill Rd.	H 7	75
Whitburn Rd.	E 6	73
Witham St.	E 6	73
Whitney Clo.	C 8	72
Whittier Rd.	D 8	73
Whittington St.	E 4	69
Whitton Clo.	H 8	75
Wicklow Rd.	G 4	70
Williams Rd., Ben.	C 4	68
Willow Av.	J 7	75
Willow Bridge Rd.,	D 4	69
Ben.		
Wiltshire Rd.	H 5	71
Winchester Av.	G 4	70
Winchester Way,	C 4	68
Scaws.		
Windermere Rd.	G 5	70
Windle Rd.	D 6	73
Windsor Rd.	F 5	70
Windsor Wk., Scaws.	C 4	68
Winterton Clo.	H 8	75
Winton Rd.	G 5	70
Wivelsfield Rd.	B 7	72
Woburn Clo.	C 8	72
Wolsey Av.	G 5	70
Wood St.	E 5	69
Woodfield Rd.	D 7	73
Woodhouse Rd.	F 4	70
Woodlea Way	H 3	71
Woods Riding	H 5	71
Woodside Rd.,	C 3	68
Scawth.		
Woodstock Rd.	C 7	72
Worcester Av.	F 3	70
Wordsworth Av.	D 8	73
Wordsworth Rd.	C 5	68
Wrightson Av., War.	B 8	72
Wrightson Ter.	E 4	69
Wroxham Way,	C 4	68
Scaws.		
Wyndthorpe Av.	J 8	75
Yarborough Ter.,	D 4	69
Ben.		
York Bar, Ben.	C 4	68
York Gdns.	H 6	75
York Rd.	D 4	69
York Rd., Scawth.	C 3	68
Young St.	E 5	69
Zetland Rd.	F 4	70

NOTES

NOTES

Albany Rd.	B03	78	Hillcrest Rd.	D02	78	Rock Pl.	C03	78
Alpine Clo.	B03	78	Hillcrest Ri.	D02	78	Royd La.	C02	78
Alpine Rd.	B03	78	Hills Rd.	C03	78	Rundle Rd.	B03	78
Armitage Rd.	C02	78	Hole House La.	B03	78	St. Andrew Rd.	D02	78
Arthur Rd.	B03	78	Hollin Busk La.	C02	78	St. Annes Rd.	C03	78
Ash Cres.	C03	78	Hollin Busk Rd.	C02	78	St. David Rd.	D02	78
Ash La.	D03	78	Hope St.	B03	78	St. George Rd.	D02	78
Ashfield Rd.	C03	78	Howson Rd.	C03	78	St. Helen Rd.	D02	78
Askew Ct.	C02	78	Hunshelf Pk.	C03	78	St. Hilda Clo.	D02	78
Beauchief	D02	78	Hunshelf Rd.	B03	78	St. Joan Av.	D02	78
Beechwood Rd.	B02	78	Jeffrey Cres.	C02	78	St. Johns Rd.	D03	78
Belmont Dr.	C03	78	John West St.	B02	78	St. Margaret Av.	D02	78
Bessemer Ter.	B03	78	Johnson St.	B03	78	St. Mark Rd.	D02	78
Birch Tree Rd.	B02	78	Kenworthy Rd.	B02	78	St. Martin Clo.	D02	78
Bocking Hill	C03	78	Knowles Av.	C02	78	St. Mary Cres.	D02	78
Bracken Moor La.	C02	78	Laburnum Gro.	B02	78	St. Mathias Rd.	D02	78
Brearley Av.	C02	78	Lancaster Rd.	B03	78	St. Patrick Rd.	D02	78
Broadhead Rd.	C03	78	Lee Av.	C03	78	St. Pauls Clo.	D02	78
Broomfield Ct.	C02	78	Lilac Av.	B02	78	St. Peter Av.	D02	78
Broomfield La.	C02	78	Lime Gro.	B02	78	St. Veronica Rd.	D02	78
Broomfield Rd.	C02	78	Linden Cres.	B03	78	Schofield Rd.	C03	78
Button Row	B03	78	Manchester Rd.	B03	78	Shay House La.	B02	78
Cambridge Rd.	D02	78	Maple Gro.	B02	78	Shay Rd.	B03	78
Carr Croft Ct.	D02	78	Marsden Rd.	C03	78	Sheldon Rd.	B03	78
Carr Fold	D02	78	Marsh St.	C03	78	Sibbering Row	D02	78
Carr Gro.	D02	78	McIntyre Rd.	B02	78	Sitwell Av.	B03	78
Carr Rd.	C02	78	Melbourne Rd.	B03	78	Smith Rd.	B03	78
Cedar Rd.	B02	78	Mill La.	D03	78	Spine Hall La.	B02	78
Chestnut Av.	B02	78	Miller St.	D03	78	Springmill Ter.	B03	78
Coal Pit La.	B02	78	Moorland Dr.	B03	78	Spurley Hey Gro.	C02	78
Cockshot La.	C02	78	Moxon Clo.	C02	78	Stanley Rd.	C02	78
Common La.	D02	78	Nanny Hill	C03	78	Stone Moore Rd.	B02	78
Coronation Rd.	B03	78	New Rd.	C03	78	Stonecliffe Dr.	B02	78
Coultos Av.	C02	78	New St.	D03	78	Sycamore Rd.	B02	78
Cull Row	D02	78	Oaks Av.	B03	78	Townend La.	D02	78
East Cres.	B03	78	Olive Rd.	B03	78	Truman Gro.	D03	78
Edward St.	B03	78	Orchard St.	D02	78	Vaughton Hill	D02	78
Ellerslie Dr.	C03	78	Oxley Clo.	B03	78	Victoria Rd.	O03	78
Ford La.	C03	78	Park Dr.	B03	78	Victoria St.	B03	78
Fox Glen Rd.	C02	78	Park Gro.	B03	78	Viola Bank	B03	78
Frank Hillock Rd.	D03	78	Park La.	C03	78	Webb Av.	D02	78
Gibson La.	B03	78	Pea Royd La.	B03	78	West Cres.	B03	78
Glebelands Rd.	C02	78	Pearson St.	B03	78	Wheatley Rd.	C03	78
Grayson Clo.	C02	78	Pennine Vw.	B02	78	Whitehead Av.	C02	78
Green St.	C03	78	Poplar Av.	B02	78	Whitwell Cres.	B03	78
Grove Rd.	D02	78	Pot House La.	B03	78	Whitwell La.	B02	78
Harvey St.	C03	78	Princess Dr.	C02	78	Willow Rd.	B02	78
Haywood Av.	C03	78	Ralph Ellis Dr.	B02	78	Wilson Rd.	D02	78
Haywood La.	C03	78	Rectory Clo.	C03	78	Wood Royd Rd.	D03	78
Haywood Rd.	C03	78	Red Fern Gro.	B02	78	Woolley Rd.	B03	78
Heath Rd.	C02	78	Ridal Av.	B03	78	Wortley Rd.	D03	78
Helliwell La.	D02	78	Robertshaw Cres.	C03	78	York Rd.	B03	78